Big Deal

The Politics of the Illicit Drug Business

Anthony Henman, Roger Lewis and Tim Malyon
with Betsy Ettore and Lee O'Bryan

Pluto Press

London and Sydney

First published in 1985 by Pluto Press Limited,
The Works, 105a Torriano Avenue, London NW5 2RX
and Pluto Press Australia Limited, PO Box 199, Leichhardt,
New South Wales 2040, Australia

7 6 5 4 3 2 1

89 88 87 86 85

22884114

Phototypeset by AKM Associates (UK) Ltd
Ajmal House, Hayes Road, Southall, Greater London
Printed in Great Britain by Guernsey Press Co. Limited
Guernsey, C.I.

British Library Cataloguing in Publication Data
Henman, Anthony
    Big deal : the politics of the illicit drug business.
    1. Narcotics, Control of——Social aspects
    2. Narcotics, Control of——Political aspects
    3. Drug abuse and crime
    I. Title
    364.1'77   HV5801

ISBN 0 7453 0008 1

Anthony Henman teaches anthropology at the University of Campinas, São Paulo. He has been conducting research into the drug-producing areas of South America since 1969 and is the author of *Mama Coca* (1979), on the cocaine business in the Andes.

Roger Lewis is an expert on the heroin trade. He is currently writing a book on the role of mafia in the drugs and arms traffic and has participated in research submitted to the Italian Antimafia Commission.

Tim Malyon is a freelance journalist and photographer. He has been investigating the cannabis market for some years and has travelled widely in South Asia and the Caribbean.

Betsy Ettore is a research sociologist at the Institute of Psychiatry, London and author of *Lesbians, Women and Society*.

Lee O'Bryan is a researcher with the Drug Indicators Project, London. He has a particular interest in youth culture and patterns of adolescent drug use.

CONTENTS

Introduction: Junkie Babies *v.*The Merchants of death □ 1

1. **Serious Business – The Global Heroin Economy** □ **Roger Lewis** □ 5
    Bad Moon Rising □ 5
    Whatever Happened to the French Connection? Heroin, Crime and Politics in the Mediterranean Basin □ 23
    Users, Dealers and Villains: The London Heroin Market in the 1980s □ 40

2. **The Cost of Lacoste – Drugs, Style and Money** □ **Lee O'Bryan** □ 50

3. **Love Seeds and Cash Crops – The Cannabis Commodity Market** □ **Tim Malyon** □ 63
    Silent Subversion □ 65
    Bibles in the Ganja Fields □ 76
    Fifteen Tons and What Did He Get? □ 95
    Appendix: Cannabis Use in Britain □ Matthew Atha and Sean Blanchard □ 103

4. Psychotropics, Passivity and the Pharmaceutical Industry □ Betsy Ettore □ 108

5. Cocaine Futures □ **Anthony Henman** □ 118
    Meet the Players: An Introduction □ 118
    Cocainism, the Highest Form of
    Imperialism? □ 124
    The Narcocracy: A Model for the Regeneration
    of Capital □ 140
    Double Standards and the Single
    Convention □ 157
    Cocaine Future □ 168

Notes □ 190
Index □ 203

Introduction:
JUNKIE BABIES v. THE
MERCHANTS OF DEATH

Merchants of death and junkie babies . . . So, big deal, what else is new?

It seems ludicrous that so little has changed in a century that prides itself on the speed of its transformations. A news cutting from the 1920s would have described 'cocaine orgies' in much the same terms as the popular press does today. You could single out from the 1960s any number of alarmist predictions about the growing threat of heroin addiction. Even in the 1980s you can still find the conservative press banging on about the brain damage caused by cannabis smoking.

Why are these formulae so pervasive? Whose interests do they serve? The monotony of the media message on the use of drugs – always described in terms of some ever-growing problem – cannot be simply the result of accident, or ignorance, or even some conspiracy to misrepresent the truth. There must be a blind spot in our culture which precludes serious discussion of the question and relegates most information on the drugs trade to the status of propaganda – used to scapegoat groups outside the mainstream of Western society, whether racial minorities, the youthful unemployed or the faceless enemy abroad.

We propose to address the illicit drugs phenomenon from a perspective which has been largely neglected. Our views on the political and economic ramifications of the business share a commitment to reporting the experiences of the actual participants in the trade – the producers, traffickers and users – rather than reiterating received wisdoms. As will become apparent, individuals and groups within the global drugs economy have widely divergent and often contradictory perspectives on current developments.

Heroin, cocaine and cannabis provide racy headlines and exotic locations. Their production is sufficiently distant to promote the idea that the threat is alien and external. Yet, the view from the producing countries is precisely the inverse. They see the drug business as something inspired by the insatiable markets of the industrialized, metropolitan world. The cocaine-producing nations of South America, for example, could legitimately begin to ask why their product has been singled out for so much bad press, when all the statistics (particularly in the UK) point to a far greater prevalence of health problems relatd to the little-publicized, domestically-produced amphetamine sulphate.

This book attempts to explore some contradictions. Are the enormous sums of money generated in the illicit drug business likely to constitute a real threat to orthodox capital? Or is speculative money moving into drugs simply on account of the dwindling prospects for rapid profit-making in a period of widespread economic stagnation?

At the end of the day, the mechanisms used by drug traffickers to launder their funds are similar to those employed by large corporate concerns to avoid tax. Attempts to trace and sequester laundered money could trigger off potentially explosive confrontations with legitimate capital as well, involving not only abstract debate about civil rights, economic privilege and the unregulated play of market forces, but also concrete scrutiny of the roles of the City of London, the Channel Islands and various Commonwealth countries as 'off shore' havens for licit and illicit funds.

Recent investigations in the United States revealed that $2 million cash in Mafia heroin profits were being laundered in carrier bag transactions on their way to Switzerland and Italy. Enforcement officials flatly stated that such sums could not be moved without the assistance of established financial institutions. Millions of dollars were traced as passing through respectable New York finance houses. When they were asked to assist in the development of inquiries, one complied, but another informed its customers. In the words of a senior enforcement official, the latter institutions 'put what we would regard as their narrow financial interest ahead of the broad public interest'.[1] It could be argued that the yields of the illicit trade, far from constituting a threat to establishment financial institutions, actually represent a new phase in the regeneration of capital.

If such is the case, what are the prospects for the future? Will the present scenario perpetuate itself, creating vested interests anxious to defend the money-making potential of the illicit market? Will corrupted narcotics enforcement forces continue to use the pretext of legal controls to target their competitors and support prices through the creation of artificial shortages? Or will governments tire of the thankless task of repressing the drugs trade and take steps to bring it out into the open where it can be taxed and regulated?

Legalization might be proposed by the United States as

a means of undermining the challenge of the illicit economy; alternatively, legalization might be advocated by Third World states to avert the bankruptcy of their governments. Whether legalized or not, the boom in the production of opium, coca and cannabis is unlikely to falter for the foreseeable future. However, a growing saturation of the market, already visible in the fall in real prices for heroin and cocaine, will inevitably develop. A decline in profit margins may lead many drugs trade entrepreneurs into new areas of investment. The groups that survive will be those who are able to establish a high degree of consumer identification for their wares. In the world of brand loyalty it matters little if the product remains illegal or not.

Or does it? The single most important point that is consistently neglected in official assessments of the illicit drugs market is the importance of illegality itself. Any serious analysis of the codes of drug consumption must recognize that a great deal of the symbolic meaning of such consumption is related to questions of legal status. It is ironic that when public service broadcasting is investing so heavily in the anti-drugs campaign, the commercial anti-heroin advertisements have to fight for billboard and airwave space against an army of legal traffickers in tobacco, caffeine and alcohol. So much for the 'war on drugs'.

1. SERIOUS BUSINESS –
THE GLOBAL HEROIN ECONOMY
Roger Lewis

'Where the big money is . . . is a matter of indifference to accumulators as long as *some* product plays that role and money can be invested in it.' (Immanuel Wallerstein, *Crisis as Transition*)

'Junk is the ideal product . . the ultimate merchandise.' (William Burroughs, *The Naked Lunch*)

Bad Moon Rising

Introduction
It is generally acknowledged that heroin use and addiction has increased significantly in Western Europe over the past ten years. All countries have been affected. Although there was a relatively minor outbreak of heroin use in the mid- and late 1960s, the heroin market was more or less contained in Britain until 1978, which appears to have been a watershed year. Since then alterations in supply, demand, modes of consumption and attitudes have determined in various ways the chain of events that were to follow. The heroin market, probably more than most, develops its own momentum.

It is interesting that a downturn in the world economy has coincided with increasing heroin consumption on a global scale. It will be even more interesting to see if heroin use peaks, stabilizes or declines if there is an economic upswing in the 1990s. Meanwhile jobs are scarce in the United Kingdom and those who have them want to hold onto them. Structural unemployment is such that a section of an entire generation has never worked and is unlikely to do so for the foreseeable future. It is at such junctures, as Gramsci might have observed, that various 'morbid symptoms' begin to appear, although their origins stem from conditions far more complex than a simple correlation between addiction and unemployment.

When the lines are drawn, what better commodity for the young, the angry, the defeated or the depressed than heroin? Whereas heroin may help to defuse or pacify potential disorder or riot, the state is hardly in a position to acknowledge the benefit of such gratuitous developments. Correlations between unemployment and addiction are played down, whilst drug scares are used to divert attention from other issues.

Amongst young users today there is often a disturbing lack of knowledge about drugs. Off-white powders are sniffed or smoked with little understanding of what they are or what they can do. There has been a widespread misapprehension that sniffing or smoking heroin will not lead to addiction. It may well not, but if you take it often enough, in whatever manner, you'll end up with a habit. It's a lovely feeling to be wrapped in that anxiety-free, cosy, cotton wool womb-with-a-view that heroin temporarily provides.

Heroin consumption is evident in all social classes. It fills differing needs as an obsessional euphoriant, analgesic, narcotic and status symbol and is used in different ways by different people. Fetishized by users and opponents alike, it is awarded a mythical status which in turn is refracted back onto the actors in the drama and used to justify their subsequent attitudes and behaviour. Heroin is used by the indolent, the wealthy, the idle rich, and the 'Chelsea brats', as well as the poor, the desperate, the homeless, the very ordinary and the generally screwed-up.

The drug tends to engender a nodded-out passivity together with sporadic but frantic activity. Demand is not as inelastic as has been claimed, but physical and psychological dependence make it far more rigid than the market demand for cannabis and cocaine. It is an ideal commodity. For the non-addicted bulk mover, there is money in it. However, in London at least you rarely meet anybody dealing heroin in small quantities who does not also have a habit. Most of their money goes on heroin. If you are using, the more you have around the more you tend to use. For some it's a living, but not a lot more.

It is a commodity for which there is a rising demand, a substantial profit at wholesale level, and a tendency toward monopoly throughout the distribution system. Monopoly rents can be extracted by importers from their suppliers, who in turn extract surplus value from the labour of primary producers and secondary technicians. Unlike suppliers of cannabis and cocaine, bulk shippers tend not to be users.

Heroin is also a popular drug. It fulfils various needs. Addicts prefer to have it if possible, but will substitute when necessary. There is no evil, organized conspiracy to import 'white death' in order to corrupt the nation's youth. There is money to be made, but to succeed the serious entrepreneur needs capital, a delivery system resistant to enforcement penetration, contacts and connections at domestic and international level, reliable employees, sufficient muscle to instil fear and deter predators, and a working knowledge of border controls, current prices and potential competition. The number of new addicts in Britain known to the Home Office rose by 50 per cent in 1982, an increasing number of whom were over 21. On the supply side, a quarter of a metric ton of heroin was seized with no discernible long-term effect on price or availability. A bulk shipment of 40 kilos was seized in a consignment of brassware at Felixstowe in May 1984, confirming that commercial freight is being used to transport increasingly large amounts of the drug. Addict notifications and the quantity of seizures continued to increase in 1983 and 1984.

The global heroin economy transcends regional and national societies, integrating a variety of activities across many parts of the world. Urban street dealing, the problems of opium farmers, and patterns of smuggling networks are not isolated, compartmentalized phenomena but links in the same chain. In order to place domestic markets and regional delivery systems in their context, it is important to look at the global picture of cultivation, production and transportation.

Bounteous harvests, heavy traffic
'Capital is said . . . to fly turbulence and strife, and to be timid, which is very true; but this is very incompletely stating the case. Capital eschews no profit, or very small profit, just as Nature was formerly said to abhor a vacuum. With adequate profit, capital is very bold. A certain 10 per cent will ensure its employment anywhere; 20 per cent will produce eagerness; 50 per cent positive audacity; 100 per cent will make it ready to trample on all human laws; 300 per cent and there is not a crime at which it will scruple, nor a risk it will not run, even to the chance

of its owner being hanged. If turbulence and strife will bring a profit, it will freely encourage both. Smuggling and the slave trade have amply proved all that is here stated.' (Marx, *Capital*, Vol. 1, p. 712)

In recent years the belief has grown both in law enforcement and in professional crime that drugs can generate profits as great as any other form of illegal enterprise. The extent of such profits are sometimes exaggerated but they are impressive by any standards.[1] Because of the difference between wholesale and retail prices, international traffickers do not receive the total 'street' value of an illicit drug. Nevertheless, the profit margins when set against labour, capital outlay and risks involved are enormous. One kilo of heroin purchased for £4,000 on the Pakistan/Afghan border may be sold as such in Britain for £20,000 to £25,000. If the kilo is sold in separate ounces it can realize between £28,000 and £42,000. Dilution or 'cutting' may increase the profits even further, although reduction of heroin content by more than half is far less common in Britain than in the United States.

At retail level the rate of profit for heroin, weight for weight, is substantially higher than for any other illicit drug, although, because of wider recreational demand, cocaine and cannabis may generate a higher overall turnover.[2] The impact of the illicit drugs economy may be perceived at its most dramatic in the revenue-raising activity of the heroin-dependent individual and, at the other end of the spectrum, in the boom of local economies geared to the traffic. Ongoing research suggests that the British heroin market in 1982 generated net profits of some £48 million.[3] Elsewhere, reports submitted to the Italian Antimafia Commission by Arlacchi and Lewis indicate that net profits generated in Naples and its hinterland alone approached £25 million in 1984.[4]

Heroin (diamorphine hydrochloride) is obtained from the opium poppy. Gum tapped from the incised poppy head after the petals have fallen is prepared, treated and morphine base chemically extracted from it. This base is subsequently mixed with acetic anhydride and converted to heroin base (diacetylmorphine) and thence into a soluble salt, diamorphine hydrochloride.[5]

With its high price, high yield per acre, labour-intensive nature and inaccessibility on high, rugged, hard-to-control terrain, opium is a tempting cash crop for impoverished tribal peoples who have successfully integrated the poppy into their domestic economy and culture. It is a low-bulk, high-value, non-perishable commodity. Income from the sale of the crop can buy guns and supplies for insurgent groups in the region (for instance, the Burmese Shan States and the Afghan border where historically imperialist and invading powers have met sustained and intractable resistance), and consumer goods and capital equipment for the cultivators themselves. Geographically close to the American market, Mexican producers have begun to employ sophisticated agricultural techniques to meet current demand – a pattern that may eventually develop elsewhere.

Although opium can be a lucrative cash crop, the peasant farmer receives, as we have seen, only a tiny fraction of what his crop will realize when converted into heroin. In early 1980 a Pathan farmer got only £22 for a kilo of opium in Pakistan, the market having been glutted by the previous year's surplus. The year before the kilo price was over £100. There were indications in 1984 that a rise in the price of raw opium might encourage farmers to further extend poppy cultivation. Ten kilos of opium convert into approximately 1.1 kilos of heroin, although this can vary according to moisture loss and morphine content which depends upon the quality of the opium. In the early 1980s one kilo of heroin could be bought on the Pakistani Northwest Frontier for £3,000 to £4,000 and even less on the Thai-Burmese border. Value increases by a factor of anything from 125 per cent to 1,000 per cent in its transition from raw material to finished product. The profit margin for the refiners is clearly substantial even after transport, refining, labour and protection costs have been deducted.[6]

American preoccupation with Turkish opium production in the early 1970s tended to overlook the production capacity of Iran, Pakistan and Afghanistan which, in conjunction with extensive political turmoil, was by the end of the decade substantial. Southeast Asia was the world's largest producer of illicit opium until 1978–79 when Southwest Asia moved into the foreground. However, Southeast Asia is once again a major source: recent estimates suggest that Burma produces 550–600 tons of raw opium per annum, and Thailand 36 tons in 1983–84. The Pakistani government claimed its own national production fell from 800 tons in 1978–9 to 44 tons in 1983–4, though 41 clandestine laboratories were seized in 1983 alone. Iran detected no illicit cultivation in 1984, firmly laying responsibility at her eastern neighbours' door.[7] Despite these claims, there appears to have been no slackening in Southwest or Southeast Asian production. 71.7 tons of opium were seized in the Near and Middle East in 1983 (86 per cent of the world total) and world seizures of heroin doubled from just over 6 tons in 1982 to almost 12 tons in 1983. The seizure of 2 tons in Europe had no noticeable impact on price at wholesale or retail level.[8]

Most claims made by governments about production and consumption have to be treated with a certain scepticism. They often have no clear idea of the situation on the ground and choose to ignore it when they have. The increasing involvement of diplomats and others of similar status in the traffic is a matter of public record. At the consumption end, Southwest Asian heroin continued to dominate the European market in 1984. After four years of good harvests, Southeast Asian heroin was also increasingly available.[9]

Development and dependence
'Heroin is our mineral wealth.' (Anonymous, Northwest Frontier Province)

Despite or perhaps because of continuing political turmoil in the poppy-growing areas of Southwest and Southeast Asia, supply, delivery and distribution systems operate with great efficiency. The poppy functions as a consistent source of hard cash and serves numerous traditional functions as well – ranging from food, fuel and fodder to euphoriant and medicine. It stores well, does not spoil, has a high value per unit weight, can be grown without fertilizer or much irrigation, and can be harvested without machinery. It is hardly surprising that attempts to suppress its cultivation encounter considerable resistance.

The most significant development in the traffic in the past ten years has been the development of a refining capacity within the poppy-growing countries of the periphery. The impact of this minor form of Third World manufacturing initiative is currently being felt in Europe. Before the 1970s Southwest Asian heroin was normally transported to the Mediterranean basin for transformation into heroin or even into morphine base. Thus, with the possible exception of prerevolutionary China, integrated production close to the growing fields is a relatively new phenomenon. By 1979 heroin and morphine base laboratories had been established in Syria, Lebanon, Pakistan, Iran, Turkey and Afghanistan.[10] Laboratories have been particularly evident in the Kurdish homelands straddling the borders of Turkey, Syria and Iraq and are now evident in India and Lebanon's Bekaa valley.

The development of a refining capacity in Afghanistan and the Northwest Frontier and Baluchi provinces of Pakistan may have taken place partly under the tutelage of European, Iranian and even Thai nationals. Capital, technical expertise and its product are not limited by national boundaries. Apparently, competition between manufacturers occurs not only in relation to prices, but also 'in respect of a greater integration which provides manufacturers having direct control over raw materials an edge on their competitors'.[11] This integration and proliferation of productive capacity, combined with increased cultivation, inevitably led to a rising supply in the 1980s. Most of the supply regions, apart from Turkey and Mexico, have strong colonial, commercial or cultural ties with Britain. Hong Kong, Britain's nineteenth-century opium staging-post to China, links into Southeast Asia, whilst Cyprus provides convenient access from Turkey and the Middle East.

The trend is clear. High-quality heroin is being refined close to its organic source in the opium fields. A series of transactions involving purchase and transportation that took place as part of the production processes between raw opium and finished hydrochloride have been eliminated, and an integrated process of production – cheap labour, reduced transport costs, plus mutual defence and security arrangements – maximizes profits. The benefits accrue primarily to the laboratory controller and the shipper who delivers direct to the consumer distribution system.

Beyond the border

The global heroin economy transcends countless states and political structures. A delicate balance of convenience exists between the enforcement of controls on the international market on the one hand, and the absence or ineffectiveness of such controls on the other. Controls have to be weak enough to permit the trade to take place, yet strong enough to eliminate excess competition and keep prices high.

Most advanced capitalist enterprises now develop complex organizational networks across national boundaries, thereby benefiting from the appropriation, processing and distribution of natural resources and exploitation of the cost advantages of different national locations.[12] As Samir Amin argues, the capitalist mode of production is based on the search for profit, quite outside any discussion of 'nation'. The bourgeoisie is *a priori* neither nationalist nor internationalist.[13] Decision-making transcends national, cultural and ethical considerations. Nowhere is this more evident than in the heroin trade.

The international trafficker takes advantage of the inability or unwillingness of peripheral states to enforce international narcotics conventions and the ability of their peripheral producing regions to successfully resist the imposition of such measures. The trader benefits simultaneously from an artificially inflated price created by international and domestic controls imposed by the consumer/core nations, the ineffectualness of such controls in impeding production and trading in the hinterland of the periphery, and the inequalities of exchange in the transference of surplus to the core from the periphery. As with other markets, the production of heroin (finished goods), morphine and heroin base (semi-finished goods), as well as the raw material (opium), increasingly takes place in the periphery to take advantage of minimal production and labour costs.

In every region of cultivation and periphery production, there is a high level of social and political non-integration of that area with the nation as a whole, and a continuing trend towards the disintegration of whatever official controls do exist. Paradoxically, as far as opium and heroin are concerned, these areas are more integrated with international market forces than they are with their own national domestic economies. Most of the tribal peoples directly involved in cultivation confer little or no legitimacy on their formally constituted rulers.

The example of Thailand shows that the strategic interests of producer nations are not necessarily served by enforcement campaigns. In encouraging a buffer region in the north between Thailand, Burma and Laos, the Thais have tended to be half-hearted in their response to trafficking warlords and former Kuomintang forces. Historically, some members of the military and governing class have also invested in the traffic.[14] Geopolitical considerations also impinge upon the government of Pakistan. The tribal territories in the Northwest Frontier provinces are still largely autonomous. Afghan opium cultivated by tribal groups in conflict with the Kabul regime is the primary source of heroin on the Pakistani border, much to the embarrassment of their US supporters:

'It is time the United States, Canada, Western Europe and the Arab countries began to demand that the Mujahideen leadership, through their mystical tribal communication network, put an end to the production of opium, morphine base and heroin in their territory as tragically affecting the countries which are their friends and benefactors'.[15]

A sustained enforcement campaign would not only alienate the fiercely independent tribal people but also destabilize the Afghan border region. Both Thailand and Pakistan prefer to retain the goodwill of their tribal residents, maintain the integrity of their admittedly porous borders and limit the possibility of local rebellion. As in other nations where opium is a traditional crop, there is little incentive rigorously to control cultivation when the hostility of growers and traders is guaranteed, direct and indirect profits are lost, and other countries would merely take up the slack. On the other hand, there is no question that the cash flow generated by the trade distorts the economies of producing countries, financing a large illicit market in otherwise unobtainable goods and services, driving up the cost of living and making life increasingly hard for those not involved in the heroin economy. Moreover, although addiction amongst the indigenous population may be exaggerated by the metropolitan nations, a number of developing countries that have recently begun to refine heroin now have growing addict populations. Iran has had a large domestic market in opium and heroin for some years and in Pakistan there are an estimated 50,000 opiate addicts in Karachi alone.[16]

Imperial legacies

'Nurtured by the East India Company, vainly combated by the Central Government at Peking, the opium trade gradually assumed larger proportions, until it absorbed about $2,500,000 in 1816 . . . In 1820, the number of chests smuggled into China had increased to 5,147; in 1821, to 7,000 and in 1824 to 12,639 . . . the opium trade increased during the ten years from 1824 to 1834 from 12,639 to 21,785 . . . in 1875 39,000 chests, valued at $25,000,000, were successfully smuggled into China, despite the desperate resistance of the Celestial Government . . . The importation was estimated in 1856 at about $35,000,000, while, in the same year, the Anglo-Indian government drew a revenue of $25,000,000, just the sixth part of its total state income, from the opium monopoly.' (Eric Williams, *Capitalism and Slavery*)

There is a frequent tendency for the metropolitan nations, particularly the USA, to blame the producer nations for the former's addiction problems. The irony is enormous, particularly given recent developments in American domestic marijuana cultivation and the seizure of at least five heroin laboratories within the United States between 1983 and 1984.[17] Intoxicants like alcohol and opium have historically facilitated the accumulation of capital and the opening up of rigid, closed societies to market forces.[18] Smuggling and contraband were part and parcel of the freebooting mercantilism upon which the industrial revolution was built. A fully-fledged market in opium did not exist in South Asia until the nineteenth century with the emergence of modern capitalism and its attendant need for labour, profits and international markets. Europe had little to offer in exchange for spices, silk and tea, apart from gold and silver. The Emperor of China wrote to George III in 1793, 'as your Ambassador can see for himself, we possess all things. I set no value on objects strange or ingenious, and have no use for your country's manufactures'.[19] Opium, like rum and guns in Africa and elsewhere, provided the key. The drug was soon being used to purchase the commodities required, to finance military expeditions, to maintain overseas territories and, for example, to provide the capital for the development of the factory system in New England in the early nineteenth century.[20]

Imperialist and ex-colonial powers having introduced or encouraged the widespread consumption of opium in the non-industrialized East to finance their own industrial take-off are now experiencing the consequences of their enterprise. The indigenous populations first integrated the poppy into the local agricultural order and then increased production in response to rising demand from the metropolis. In the past, the metropolitan powers used military means to impose the opium traffic on resistant nations. Today, insurgent involvement in trafficking is invoked as justification for intervention in the internal affairs of sovereign nations.[21]

General trade relations between the industrial core nations and the periphery profoundly determine the development and structure of the opiate traffic. Almost all countries illicitly producing opium on a significant scale are underdeveloped ones. The farmers tend to be politically marginal members of ethnic minorities living off subsistence economies and subject to 'alien' rule. Opium guarantees a sufficient income for daily survival and a limited amount of hard cash when required. As long as they have no access to more adequate sources of income, they will continue to cultivate the poppy. Terrain and climate are inappropriate for most other crops, which in any case would generate less income. This concentration distorts the local economy as it becomes increasingly dependent on one product. Local economic survival entails the continued cultivation and export of a single crop, this economic 'push' factor giving additional propulsion to the trade.[22] A pattern of primary producers suffering from distorted economies has been an inherent feature of the relationship between the advanced capitalist countries and the periphery. Altering the pattern would entail altering the entire economic order. Until that happens, given current patterns of global consumption and production, it looks as though the heroin trade is here to stay.

Estimated production of opium in Southwest Asia, 1979–83; weights in metric tons (UN Commission on Narcotic Drugs)

Country	1979	1980	1981	1982	1983
Iran	300	400–600	400–600	400–600	400–600
Afghanistan	270–300	200	225	250–300	400–575
Pakistan	800	125	85–100	75	63
Total	1,370–1,400	725–925	710–925	725–925	863–1,238

Estimated production of opium in Southeast Asia, 1979–83; weights in metric tons (UN Commission on Narcotic Drugs)

Country	1979	1980	1981	1982	1983
Burma	150–170	500–550	500	500	500–600
Laos	40	50	50	50	30–40
Thailand	10–15	50	50–60	47–50	30–35
Total	200–225	600–650	600–610	597–600	560–675

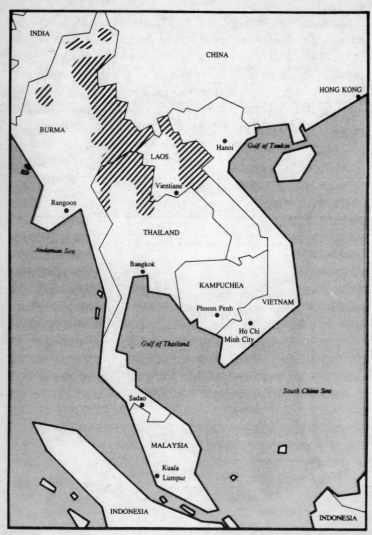

Opium poppy-growing areas in the Golden Triangle region of Southeast Asia, 1983 (Royal Canadian Mounted Police, National Drug Intelligence Estimate, 1983)

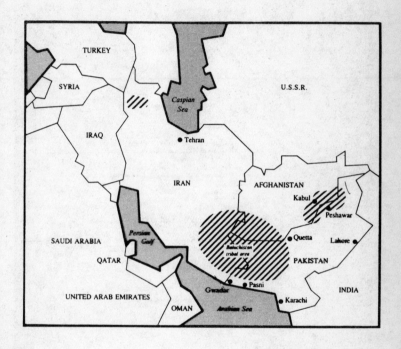

Opium poppy-growing areas in the Golden Crescent regions of Southwest Asia, 1983 (Royal Canadian Mounted Police, National Drug Intelligence Estimate, 1983)

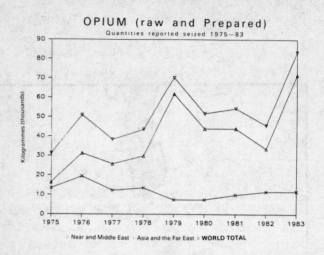

OPIUM (raw and Prepared)
Quantities reported seized 1975—83

Near and Middle East · Asia and the Far East ▷ **WORLD TOTAL**

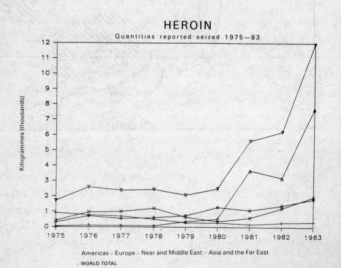

HEROIN
Quantities reported seized 1975—83

Americas ▷ Europe ▷ Near and Middle East · Asia and the Far East
· **WORLD TOTAL**

**Whatever Happened to the French Connection?
– Heroin, Crime and Politics in the Mediterranean Basin**

'Received opinion in Marseilles was that the best government was the one that gave speculators the most room to move in.' (Emile Zola, 1867)

'He who has money and friends has justice by the tail.' (Sicilian proverb)

Introduction
French and Italian heroin trafficking structures have been consistently directed at the United States since World War II, although there has been increasing spillage onto the Italian domestic market since 1978. They are worth looking at because of their classic nature, their notoriety, their political implications and the relative abundance of documentary evidence. A detailed study shows how the trafficking structures grew with the changing political role played by France and, in particular, by Marseilles. The city came into its own in the post-World War II period when the US-dominated Marshall Plan called forth a political elite to administer the measure of economic reflation the Plan provided for.

Franco-Corsican domination of the American market in heroin during the 1960s and early 1970s was rooted in political alliances cemented during World War II and even earlier; alliances utilized to maintain the status quo at home and in the pursuit of private interest at home and abroad. The political control of Marseilles, colonial wars in Indochina and Algeria, the security of the Gaullist state, intelligence activities directed at foreign enemies and ostensible allies, and the neglect of Corsica itself, all these played a part in the growth and resilience of the French manufacturing and delivery system.

French heroin refining originated in legitimate laboratories which in the 1920s also began to supply the illicit market. Illicit production subsequently shifted from Paris to Marseilles to escape stricter pharmaceutical controls and obtain the advantages of a regional underworld directly linked to opium and morphine base producers in the Near and Far East.[1]

At the time, Marseilles crime was dominated by François Spirito and Bonaventre Carbone, the political allies and muscle of Simon Sabiani, the city's right-wing Deputy Mayor. Spirito and Carbone, whose interests in Mediterranean and Near-Eastern prostitution were extensive, organized the opiate trade on a systematic import-export basis, dealing directly with producers and carefully monitoring transport routes.[2]

The Guerini brothers, who had fought the pro-Fascist Spirito and Carbone in pre-war Marseilles on behalf of the socialist interest, supplanted their rivals in 1945. With the tacit approval of the city's socialist establishment, they harassed Communist and trade union militants, broke picket lines, and with covert American funding eased the arrival of Marshall plan goods and, later, the shipment of arms to Indochina. Their amicable relations with the city administration and their presence on the docks coincided with increased Mafia demand for new sources of heroin. Licit Italian supplies purchased by Salvatore Lucania – Charlie 'Lucky' Luciano – for shipment to the US had dried up by the mid-1950s and illicit refining operations in Italy were also being disrupted.[3]

Marseilles, one of Europe's largest ports, with a nearby

perfume industry using large quantities of acetic anhydride necessary for the synthesis of heroin, had connections for raw materials, a disinterested, even friendly, administration, a large Corsican milieu combining cosmopolitan sophistication with a clannish attachment to traditional values of silence and honour, and eager customers with direct links to American bulk buyers. Contraband was a way of life. The city was to be a prime source of top-quality heroin for the next 20 years.

The most significant development during this period was the shift in organizational balance between the French and the Mafia. Because the links between Sicilian and Italian-American families were so strong, there had been an initial tendency for French heroin to be shipped to Naples, Genoa, and Palermo where it would be purchased by the Italians and forwarded to the United States. One French trafficker confided to an undercover agent that he would be prepared to pay any price to discover how the Sicilians effected their deliveries.[4] However, by the early 1960s French groups were dealing directly with American buyers in Mexico, Canada and the United States.

US Senate reports published in the mid-1960s identified Marcel Francisci, Nick Venturi and the irrepressible Spirito as major suppliers to the United States, the latter moving as many as 50 kilos per month. Montreal was a favoured transit point for the French, although a southern route via Mexico was also developed. Prior to 1950, most heroin had entered the US directly through New York.

Until the mid-1960s the French had depended upon middlemen in the Lebanon to obtain Turkish morphine base. Eventually, direct links were forged with base suppliers as had been done with purchasers of the finished product. In consequence, the opportunity arose to construct integrated organizations that could move morphine base directly from Turkey to Marseilles, refine it into heroin, arrange transportation to the United States and make connections with Italian-American bulk buyers. Direct Franco-Turkish trade was assisted by Armenian members of the Marseilles underworld who were able to negotiate with the vendors in their own language.

The 'quiet men', who oversaw the trade, were facilitators. They usually never saw the drug, but at every stage of the route took a commission from buyers, couriers and sellers, franchises or percentage investments being offered on particular shipments.[5] By the end of the 1960s the French underworld was keenly aware of the large profits to be made from heroin smuggling and a variety of freelance groups emerged to cash in on the boom.[6]

Despite the insularity of the Marseilles milieu, the trade became increasingly chaotic as indiscreet and less competent freelancers formed short-lived groups to exploit demand in a scramble that has been likened to a gold rush. An even more ferocious form of competition manifested itself in Palermo in the early 1980s as Mafia families fought for control of the business. Individuals 'buying into' consignments sometimes succeeded in setting up secondary networks on the strength of their proceeds. However, the co-ordination of bulk financing and refining remained the prerogative of a relatively select few. In 1970 a kilo of heroin purchased in Marseilles for $2,000 could be sold in New York for $12,000; costs were $1,000 for the courier and $1,000 for expenses.[7]

Major figures maintained links with Turkey and the United States ran their own laboratory, sold heroin to small teams of couriers and arranged buyers in the United

States. They took 10 per cent of the value of the cargo from the transportation teams and a 10 per cent commission from the buyers. Shares were taken out on each consignment – a kilo for someone who was owed a favour, a kilo for a prisoner's dependents and so on.[8]

Despite revelations in late 1984 about the formal organization of Mafia relations by Tommaso Buscetta, a former high-ranking Sicilian heroin trafficker, organized crime is far less rigid and monolithic than most people suppose.[9] The Corsican and Marseilles milieu are bound by a common cultural heritage, kinship ties and their own style of operating rather than by the formal regulations of a rigid organization. There has been speculation about the continuing existence of a secret Union Corse, which certainly seems to have functioned as a cultural and resistance organization during the German occupation.

The interplay of relationships within heroin networks is as much dependent on past associations, friendships and potential profit margins as it is on an immutable criminal hierarchy. A financier's or wholesaler's capacity to induce fear, loyalty and respect serves little purpose unless it is combined with business acumen and organizational ability. However, entrepreneurial aggressiveness unhindered by the constraints of legality tends to succeed until checked by equally ruthless rivals, as in the Sicilian Mafia war of 1980–83, or committed intervention by the state, armed metaphorically and literally with superior resources.

Pressure and fragmentation
The Marseilles milieu is a relatively closed world and there was little political will to intervene on the part of the French government until the early 1970s. It was primarily American pressure, heightened by Nixon's self-proclaimed

'war on drugs', and the vulnerability and incompetence of one-off trafficking teams that created a climate for change. The American tendency to externalize problems and seek solutions abroad was reinforced by the erroneous view that drugs were the cause of most street crime and that their elimination might influence the 1972 presidential election. In Washington there was talk of 'clandestine law enforcement' and 'eliminating' foreign traffickers who enjoyed police immunity or protection in their own country. Whereas Egil Krogh, high-ranking White House drugs strategist of the period, claims that the only killings occurred in Southeast Asia where the CIA arranged for various traffickers to trap their enemies, his assistants have intimated that further steps were taken that directly disruped the French-supplied Latin-American connection.

325 kilos of heroin were seized in France in 1970, 755 kilos in 1971 and 811 kilos in 1972, most of which was intended for the USA. Given that a single lab could produce 75 to 150 kilos within one to two weeks using an overlapping batch process, the quantities seized were probably less important than the closing down of networks as a result of such seizures.[10] At the height of the campaign the US were monitoring at least 2,000 phone calls per week, and $50,000 rewards were on open offer in Marseilles itself.[11]

The first public expression in France of American irritation at French lassitude and even complicity came in August 1971 when John Cusack, director of the Bureau of Narcotic and Dangerous Drugs (BNDD) European operation, declared that 'thanks to their bank balances, special connections and consideration shown them' certain 'big fish' were untouchable.[12] Having forcefully made his point, Cusack was recalled at the request of the French government.

There is little doubt that major traffickers benefited from their links with various elements within the nation's power structure. One senior Interpol official commented privately to the author that the litany of scandal and corruption involving the police, French crime and politics would never be entirely eliminated until those politicians and public figures compromised by alliances made both in collaborationist and resistance circles during the Vichy period were dead.

Marcel Francisci, a prominent Corsican businessman with extensive gambling interests, would have been very much in Cusack's mind when he complained of French inertia. A Gaullist sympathizer since the war, Francisci became firm friends with a number of rising politicians who attained prominence after de Gaulle took power. During the 1950s he developed business interests throughout the Mediterranean. He ran a gambling club in Beirut, a major crossroads in illegal trading for arms and drugs, both fundamental components of the international traffic in illicit commodities. Some years later he tried and failed to extend his gambling interests to London.[13] Having emerged victorious from a Parisian gambling war in the 1960s, he was shot dead in an underground carpark in 1982.

In the late 1960s Francisci was rumoured to be a key figure insulated from any direct trafficking associations – a financier, fixer and arranger, who had ousted the Guerinis from their former preeminent position in the French underworld. Following American denunciations in 1971, a certain distancing of ministerial contacts ensued. Evidence clearly suggests that Francisci was a central organizing figure as the 'French Connection' came to a peak in the 1960s.[14] The Pelletier Report to the French government[15] specifically comments that the general public during this period was genuinely convinced that the police were prepared to arrest users but left serious traffickers alone because of the protection that they were afforded.

Despite the resistance credentials of traffickers with ties to the Gaullist and socialist camps, they had few scruples about dealing with former Nazi collaborators. Business was business. Auguste Ricord, a pre-war associate of Spirito and Carbone recruited by the Gestapo in 1941, fled to South America after the war. By the early 1960s he was busy assembling a Latin-American heroin network in Stroessner's Paraguay, a haven for smugglers and bolt hole for Nazi war criminals. [16] With an estimated turnover of $2.5 million per year, he seemed invulnerable. In the early 1970s, he was finally and controversially extradited to the US only after Paraguay was threatened with a $5 million credit loss and political destabilization that would discredit Ricord.

Colonial wars, honourable correspondents and the Service d'Action Civique (SAC)

In 1948 the administration officially decided to discourage opium production in French-controlled Indochina. Coincidentally, French intelligence, short of funds for their clandestine war against the Viet Minh, rapidly took control of the Indochinese traffic which they effectively dominated by 1951. The Binh Xuyen river pirates were allowed to run a variety of illicit enterprises in return for hard cash and political loyalty. This included the distribution of opium in Saigon and Cholon under the supervision of the Deuxième Bureau at the retail end of what became known as Operation X. Sanctioned at the highest level by the Service de Documentation et de Contre-Espionage (SDECE) and General Raoul Salan, the operation reached its peak between 1951 and 1954. The Binh Xuyen so successfully countered Viet Minh advances in Saigon that it is hardly surprising that President Diem resorted to a similar formula by reviving the opium trade in 1958 against American wishes.[17]

The Delouette case, more than any other, drew international attention to the kind of personnel employed by SDECE, the French secret service. Roger Delouette was arrested in 1971 at Port Elizabeth, New Jersey, on the point of taking delivery of 44.5 kilos of heroin concealed in a VW camper shipped from Le Havre. According to Delouette, the shipment had been arranged by a high-ranking officer of SDECE and his instructions had been carried out to the letter. A transatlantic polemic ensued as the French attempted to discredit Delouette and obscure his SDECE credentials.[18] As the case broke, a SDECE official admitted to the press that criminal elements were sometimes used by the agency for 'dirty tricks' as well as to generate and multiply income 20 or 30 fold, the agents being accorded 'certain facilities' in compensation.[19] The arrest of heroin trafficker André Labay, whose secret service connections had never been denied, also gave Delouette's story a level of credibility. Given Franco-American feuding and feuding within SDECE itself, Delouette seems to have been a puppet on a very long piece of string involved in events beyond his control or comprehension. Oddly enough, the officer named had served in Vietnam at the time of Operation X and later conducted research on the CIA's suspected role in the

Southeast Asian opium traffic.

The origins of the Service d'Action Civique (SAC) lay in the 'service d'ordre' of the Gaullist party in the immediate postwar period. It was kept for some of the dirtiest jobs that SDECE or the military could not or would not handle. In the late 1940s the Gaullists were able to call on 16,000 men, some of them young criminals, in an organization created by politicians who, ten years later, were to take power with de Gaulle in the Fifth Republic.

In 1970 Raymond Marcellin, the Interior Minister of the day, declared that 'a large number of heroin traffickers were recruited among the members of SAC'.[20] Later, in a remarkably forthright statement made when Corsican politicians were closing ranks against mounting criticism, the Ajaccio Junior Chamber of Commerce observed that the heroin traffic was not possible without a measure of political protection. 'Politicians of all shades and opinions, in Corsica as elsewhere, were accustomed to protecting themselves during their electoral campaigns with under-world figures. Once the campaign was over, yesterday's protected in their turn became protectors.'[21]

The need for campaign muscle and specialists in unconventional action did not evaporate with the triumph of Gaullism. SAC and the Marseilles milieu were used successively to combat Algerian nationalism, the Organisation de l'Armée Secrète (OAS) and student and leftist unrest. SAC was formally established in 1958 and pitted against the Algerian Front de Libération Nationale (FLN).[22]

The decline of SAC coincided in part with the decline of the French Connection. When Pompidou became president he effected a purge and Giscard d'Estaing felt he could do without SAC's assistance during his own presidential campaign. Its influence was much diminished by late 1975. However, scandals involving SAC, including a particularly bloody family killing near Marseilles, continued to recur until its abolition following government hearings in the early 1980s.[23]

End of an era
The last major convictions in the 'Connection' series were obtained in 1978. The accused pleaded their age, respectability, family, the Mediterranean environment and vindictive foreign pressure, describing home lives very different from that of the despised street junkie. The irony was not entirely lost on their audience.[24] Some unconvicted traffickers died in gang warfare. Others, possessing an intimate knowledge of the traffic and suspected of betrayal, were murdered in prison.[25]

Sustained enforcement pressure, a temporary ban on poppy cultivation in Turkey, alternative heroin supplies from Mexico and Southeast Asia, the rise of Latin and black wholesalers with Asian and Mexican connections and the withdrawal of protection in France under changing political conditions, all these had undermined French marketing networks by 1974. Although the French managed to supplant Mafia exporters for two decades, the Sicilians had tighter links with their American cousins and by the late 1970s had more than recouped the advantage they had lost.

Heroin manufactured in France in the 1950s and 1960s was rarely distributed on the domestic market. Lack of demand, high American prices and fears of provoking a political and judicial backlash were the determining factors rather than patriotism and moral scruples. The foreign dimension doubtless assisted others in looking the other way. The most intense period of French production and export occurred at a time when public officials were prepared to turn a blind eye to the activities of individuals providing an auxiliary 'policing' service for prominent politicians and the Gaullist state. In Marseilles these elements conveniently had links with the city's socialist administration as well.

It was sufficient that only a small section of the political and administrative class occupying focal positions within the infrastructure closed their eyes to the traffic. French trafficking expertise, the quality of their product and the influence and power that they wielded, enabled key traders to deal with Italian-American crime on an equal basis and supplant Mafia production and exportation to the United States for some 20 years.

The French police have tended to emphasize the freelance nature of the traffic with its shifting alliances and isolated participants. In fact, the literature is full of connections and coincidences involving various groups of traffickers that link operators to one another in a manner resembling a venereal disease outbreak or a street heroin subculture. Ramifications from separate cases overlap and tie in with other investigations and inquiries. It would be impossible to establish an operation in Marseilles that was entirely independent of existing morphine base suppliers, laboratories and distribution networks. Only the shadowy financiers and bankers seem able to seal themselves from the various stages in the traffic, thanks to a law of silence, their capacity for retaliation, and the protection of old and valued associates.

Given the expertise of the French secret service, it seems unbelievable that SDECE would not have heard of the activities of 'honourable correspondents' involved in the traffic. Either SDECE was one of the most incompetent and inefficient intelligence agencies in the world or it chose for sectional or venal interests to look the other way. Despite other priorities, its sheer lack of interest is quite staggering. As regards SAC, apart from their regular employment of known criminals and traffickers, questions have been raised about certain forms of fund raising. Similar questions have been raised in the past about SDECE as they have been about the CIA's former allies in Southeast Asia.

National and regional government in France was penetrated at various levels during this period by representatives of a criminal economy that often ran parallel to legitimate business enterprise. The French underworld did much to preserve the Gaullist state between 1958 and 1970, although its corrupting influence composed an obvious threat to the ideology and institutions of the state. Lessons learned about the French Connection can be usefully applied to analyse other smuggling networks, other economies and other commodity markets.

Marseilles, Palermo and the Sicilian heroin war
'Look, what interests me is the "primitive accumulation" of mafia capital, the recycling of dirty money, the stolen lire . . .' (General Dalla Chiesa, Prefect of Palermo, 27 days before his assassination on 3 September 1982)

In 1974 Judge Pierre Michel was appointed investigating magistrate in Marseilles. He was never convinced that the French Connection was entirely dead and spearheaded investigations into the French contribution to burgeoning Sicilian production in the late 1970s, collaborating closely with Italian colleagues. French access to Turkish morphine base and French refining skills contributed significantly to the resurgence of the Sicilian production industry. At home, Michel successfully closed down five French laboratories in the space of two years, and participated in the inquiry that netted the first Sicilian laboratory since 1948, resulting in the capture of Gerlando Alberti, a powerful and notorious Mafia trafficker. Michel was subsequently assassinated in Marseilles in October 1981.[26]

The killing of public figures – judges, government officials, senior police officers, investigative journalists and anti-Mafia politicians – in defence of profits, primarily heroin profits, and the political system that facilitates their accrual, has occurred in Sicily with increasing regularity since 1977. Although the French Connection at its height exploited its contacts with public figures and institutions for its own ends, its official collaborators never surrendered control to their criminal associates. In Palermo the Mafia controls the entire construction industry, much of the public administration, and kills where and when it pleases. Whereas in the past its influence was built on 'respect' for traditional values, 'the scrawny monopolies based on scarcity',[27] mediation and the threat of violence, its economic power in the past 15 years has been built to a large extent on heroin. The contemporary Mafia is an enterpreneurial Mafia, a business Mafia, entrenched within the private and public sectors of the national and Sicilian economy. Its heroin interests are, of course, international.

As French heroin production tailed off in the early 1970s, a number of laboratories were established in Sicily capable of supplying a significant proportion of the US market. In 1979 there were known to be five laboratories on the island, each subdivided between different families, with a potential production capacity of 50 kilos per week.[28] At $100,000 per kilo on delivery, the rate of profit has been compared to that achieved by shipowners engaged in the seventeenth-century slave trade. It has been estimated that in Palermo 30,000 citizens benefit directly from the traffic.[29]

In April 1983 the author and Reuters correspondent Michael Sheridan were informed without any prompting by the proprietor of a smart Palermo restaurant that his business was suffering because of the crackdown on heroin. Exactly such fears were expressed by wealthy Palermitans when General Dalla Chiesa was appointed prefect of the city in April 1982. Within 100 days he and his wife were gunned down with the same Kalashnikov rifle that had been used to eliminate the leaders of the 'losing' factions in the 1980–83 Mafia war. Dalla Chiesa's son angrily accused the Sicilian Christian-Democrat leadership of the moral authorship of the crime, even if the trigger was pulled by gunmen from Catania acting for the Corleone, Catanesi and Greco Mafia grouping.[30]

Although the murderous conflict that rent Sicily in the early 1980s was part of a wider struggle for economic and territorial hegemony between various Mafia groupings, it could be called a 'heroin war'. The struggle broke out following the breaking of a trafficking operation controlled by the Spatola, Inzerillo, Bontade and Gambino families. The grouping had grown immensely wealthy from the production and supply of high-quality heroin to their relatives in the New York Gambino family. Although many families shared laboratories and took percentage shares on consignments, the Corleonesi and the Greco family, traditional heavyweights in Mafia affairs and the drug traffic, resented the wealth, ascendancy, supposed double-dealing and apparent incompetence of the Bontade/Inzerillo grouping. In combination with the Santapaola family of Catania, they embarked upon a war that took 122 lives in Palermo in 1981, 250 lives in 1982, and 123 lives in 1983.[31] Inevitably, subsidiary vendettas erupted and the weeks were punctuated by atrocious killings and disappearances. The 'losing' faction was effectively destroyed.

The arrogance of the Mafia was such that they felt capable not only of pursuing a fratricidal war without quarter but of simultaneously attacking and killing senior representatives of the local and national state. Paradoxically, heroin gave them economic strength but was also their Achilles' heel. In April 1984, Gaetano Badalamenti, a former head of the Sicilian Mafia's Interprovincial Commission and ally of the 'losing' faction, was arrested in Madrid where he had taken refuge and was conducting business. He was charged with supplying heroin valued at $1.65 billion over a five-year period to the North American Bonanno family, and is currently awaiting trial.

Strategically placed as Sicily is between Southwest Asian morphine base suppliers and US customers, the global heroin economy provided immense financial opportunities through refining and transportation. However, its international nature and the astronomical sums involved created serious logistical and administrative problems. Within Sicily itself and the political and economic sectors that they controlled, the Mafia were almost invulnerable. However, market conditions were such that they were forced to rely upon French chemists, foreign couriers, North American customers and transnational financial speculators to refine, transport and purchase their heroin and to launder, repatriate and recycle their profits. None of these individuals, not even their American cousins, subscribed to the same codes and constraints that they would expect from their own family members. They were let down by their chemists, penetrated and betrayed by their couriers, dogged by international law enforcement, and, with an embarrassing excess of liquid capital, exploited by bankers and speculators like Michele Sindona.

At the same time, the killing of figures like Dalla Chiesa, Judge Rocco Chinnici, Judge Ciaccio Montalto and the recent attempt on the life of Judge Carlo Palermo, in which a mother and young twins died, enraged and exasperated public opinion. The Church, in Sicily traditionally mute on Mafia matters, denounced them. The Christian Democrat party, an historical ally, was defensive and divided, and finally in 1984, the former mayor of Palermo, Vito Ciancimino and the influential financiers and backers were arrested. In the spring of 1985, Giovanni Falcone, a frontline magistrate with an armour-plated Alfa and 22 bodyguards, told the press that he was still hoping for the best, but prepared for the worst. There was a clear implication that the governing political class was afraid of further revelations. Investigating magistrates felt increasingly abandoned by the state. Inquiries were encroaching upon the higher reaches of government, politics and finance – areas where the milieu in France had barely a toehold. The Italian investigators, encouraged by US colleagues possibly unaware of the potential consequences, were following the money and, in the context of the global heroin economy, that could lead anywhere.

Users, Dealers and Villains —
the London Heroin Market in the 1980s

'Happiness might now be bought for a penny, and carried in the waistcoat pocket.' (Thomas De Quincey, *Confessions of an English Opium Eater*)

While the illegality of heroin has determined the manner of distribution and consumption of the drug in both the US and Europe, the European experience has been different for geographical, historical and political reasons. Most accounts of the heroin phenomenon tend to concentrate on international trafficking deals or the anguish and degradation of the individual addict, they fail to take into consideration the heroin market in both its national and international dimensions. By so doing they take the spotlight off the powerful financial forces that dominate the market.

An illicit market in heroin has been evident in Britain since the mid-1960s when six pills (64 milligrams), could be purchased illegally for £1.[1] Until 1968 this 'grey' market was almost entirely in legitimately prescribed, 100 per cent pure heroin that was subsequently sold or exchanged for cash, goods or other drugs. It was neither legitimate nor entirely criminalized. After 1968 a black market in illicitly imported heroin gradually developed. Following a restructuring of the treatment system, the price of pharmaceutical heroin on the illicit market trebled to £3 for 64 milligrams. The price of 'Chinese' heroin also began to rise as the availability of pharmaceutical heroin diverted from legitimate sources diminished.[2]

Sustained cutbacks in legitimate supplies of heroin to addicts in the early 1970s occurred at a time when international developments in Western Europe and Southeast Asia had led to increased imports of illicit heroin into London and other European cities. Since then continuing shifts and adjustments in patterns of production, delivery and consumption have meant that no single source, legitimate or otherwise, has dominated the market at consumer level, despite a tendency to monopoly throughout the distribution system.

Product Differentiation
At first, illicitly imported supplies consisted largely of granular, grey or pinkish 'No. 3' heroin, resembling cat litter in appearance. This smoking preparation of 30–45 per cent purity was increasingly replaced in the mid 1970s by a fine, white, powdery Southeast Asian 'No. 4' heroin of significantly higher purity.[3] By 1977, the retail price had risen to £75 per gram.[4] 'Brand loyalty' to Southeast Asian 'No. 4' or 'Thai' heroin still persists and, when available, its price is correspondingly high. A dark, brown, chunky form of heroin intended for smoking (like Southeast Asian 'No. 3') was available in Iranian student circles in 1975;[5] by 1978–9, given a marked decline in Southeast Asian supplies, there was a ready demand for 'Iranian' heroin.

Persistent reports and retrospective comments from users in 1980 strongly suggest that 1978–9 was a watershed year for heroin use in Britain. Political events in Iran itself contributed to a substantial increase in supply on the British market. It was evident by mid–1979 that some wealthy Iranian exiles, particularly in London and Los Angeles, were moving their capital in the form of heroin rather than gold or other commodities. The involvement of SAVAK and members of the Iranian ruling elite in the traffic had been rumoured for some years, both in Iran and Western Europe.

This increase in availability led to a fall in price which, combined with a decline in subcultural taboos against heroin use, filled existing demand and seemed to encourage experimentation, thereby generating new demand.[6] By the end of the 1970s, there was an established and growing black market in imported heroin in the United Kingdom. Its growth was accompanied by the increased involvement of professional criminals.[7]

Since 1977 the market has been increasingly dominated by heroin manufactured in Southwest Asia; initially Iranian, subsequently Turkish and, by 1982, primarily Pakistani in origin.[8] The increasing domination of the market by Pakistan seems to have created a situation in which distinctions made by consumers between types of heroin based on national origin are becoming less common. This may be no bad thing, given the tendency of the press to see the trade in terms of unscrupulous foreigners dumping 'white death' on innocent British kids rather than as an articulated world economy. The role of ethnic minorities in deliveries to Britain has involved only a tiny proportion of mainly professional criminals, international entrepreneurs with appropriate cultural, linguistic and regional connections, diplomats with privileged status, and small-time couriers/ importers responding to illegal economic demand.

Ready availability, an attractive price, subcultural familiarity with and sometimes acceptance of use, have made heroin the drug of preference for most casual, regular and dependent opioid users in London and other parts of the country.[9] The only legitimately manufactured heroin on the black market now comes either in the form of freeze-dried ampoules diverted from prescriptions or as pharmaceutical heroin powder stolen, like some ampoules, from pharmacies and warehouses.

Heroin in Britain is measured in both metric and avoirdupois units. At point of import, bulk consignments are measured in kilograms. Further down the distribution chain, at what could be described as routine wholesale level, heroin is purchased in ounce or multigram amounts and, subsequently, sold to consumers in retail quantities. Weighed quantities at retail level take the form of gram or fraction of a gram units. At the lowest and least quantifiable level of retail distribution, heroin is sold in £5 and £10 bags. One might expect a £10 bag to weigh approximately one-tenth of a gram, but the opportunities for deception at this level, where the product comes ready-wrapped, are considerable.

Heroin purchased in wholesale quantities is much cheaper than heroin purchased in single gram or milligram units. Between 1980 and mid-1983 retail prices were almost double those of wholesale prices. Since 1981 bag purchases (£5 and £10 packets) have become increasingly prominent at retail level and are no longer limited to the 'street scene'.

Open-air trading is essentially restricted to a few parts of central London, such as Piccadilly Circus, High Street Kensington, Earls Court and King's Cross. Many 'semi-public' places, like pubs or clubs and some housing complexes also host active trading. However, most transactions, wholesale and retail, take place behind closed doors.

Demand, delivery and distribution

Dealers or suppliers trading in amounts of less than an ounce are almost always heroin users and, invariably, addicted. Ready access to cheap heroin is a constant temptation to the using, but as yet non-addicted, dealer. Much of the profit made by addicted dealers is consumed in the form of heroin. Similarly, habits may be supported or subsidized by users by supplying friends at a slight mark-up on cost. Partners or friends may assist full-time dealers to operate their business by 'running', stashing and holding drugs or coping with customers and are often paid in heroin for such services.

Despite enormous variations within individual trans-actions, relatively standard practices do occur with regards to product and price negotiation. Most people in the trade (users and dealers) have some idea of what is deemed a fair price at the level within which they are operating, despite real difficulties in assessing value for money.

Given that the price per gram at retail/consumer level currently tends to be twice that at wholesale ounce level, there is a high rate of return on transactions at one remove from consumer level. However, the big money is at the kilo end of the market, dominated by the non-addicted professional entrepreneur.

The illegality of heroin, restricted access to market information, and the physiological and/or psychological dependence that many consumers have are consonant with a tendency to monopoly throughout the distribution system. However, the product does not inevitably take precedence over all other wants and necessities. Users may abstain, substitute other drugs for heroin, seek treatment or explore other supply sources rather than pay monopoly prices. Heroin may be the drug of preference but it is not necessarily the drug consumed.

Price fluctuations are likely to affect the consumption patterns of intermittent users who take heroin for recreational purposes, as well as those of individuals dependent upon the drug. The point at which a fluctuation in price affects individual response will depend upon the economic status and circumstances of the individual concerned. There are limits beyond which the user cannot or will not go. The stereotype of the crazed, enslaved junkie prepared to commit any crime to get their fix just does not hold.

Dilution, price and purity

American studies suggest that a restriction in supply accompanied by a price increase may be followed by a decline in purity as distributors attempt to pass increased costs on to the consumer.[10] Heroin on the British market has been of relatively high quality since the 1960s 'grey' market in pharmaceutically pure heroin tablets. London has a relatively direct and casual delivery system compared to that of New York where, historically, extensive demand has led to extended and multilayered distribution dominated by a few organized crime families and a limited number of independent importers.[11]

Since 1968 increased demand in Britain has been met, firstly, by an opioid-prescribing treatment system providing heroin substitutes and strictly limited supplies of pharmaceutical heroin; and, secondly, by an illicit market in high-quality heroin delivered directly from regions with established trading, cultural and colonial relations with the United Kingdom. This has meant that dilution played and continues to play a far less pronounced role in Britain than it has in America. The quality and quantity of current supplies suggests that this will continue to be the case.

On average, purity at point of import into Britain is in the region of 70 per cent and retail purity in the region of 45–55 per cent. The purity of individual samples can vary enormously. Over the period 1980–84, declining prices have been matched by steadily rising purity.[12] The mean (reported) retail price of heroin rose from £71 per gram at the end of 1980 to £85 per gram in the second half of 1981, subsequently falling to £72 per gram in 1983. The wholesale price rose from £36 per gram in 1980 to peak at £48 per gram in the first half of 1982, falling to £34 per gram in the second half of 1983.

The fall in retail prices from the beginning of 1982 onwards probably reflects an increase in availability, which subsequently led wholesalers to reduce their prices in order to remain competitive with other suppliers. Such an interpretation is supported by anecdotal reports early in 1982 that heroin was very readily available in the metropolis. By the first half of 1983, the wholesale price at £34 per gram was slightly lower than it had been in 1980, while the retail price in 1981 and 1983 was almost identical. In relation to inflation, using the Department of Employment's general index of retail prices on all items as a deflator, the retail price of heroin fell in real terms by almost 20 per cent between the last quarter of 1980 and the second quarter of 1983, while the wholesale price fell in the region of 25%.[13] These findings by Lewis and others confirmed later assessments by the United Nations that illicit heroin prices in Western Europe generally fell by as much as 25 per cent between 1980 and 1983. In a few cases the decrease was even more marked, despite a 40 per cent increase in reported seizures over the same period.[14]

The highest prices paid for heroin were for those samples with the highest perceived strength and lowest perceived level of impurity. Dark-brown, 'Iranian' smoking heroin, for example, although frequently high in opioid content, is crudely refined and can cause particular problems in preparing for injection. It frequently requires acidification, which may be achieved by adding citric acid to the material to render its base content soluble for injection purposes. Pharmaceutical and high-quality white, Southeast Asian No. 4 (or 'Thai') heroin is much valued because it is seen as pure, strong and relatively 'clean'. Pharmaceutical heroin was retailing for as much as £110 per gram in the summer of 1981 and so-called 'Thai' for £120 in the spring of the same year. On occasions 'Pakistani' heroin was of such a high quality that it was mistaken for 'Thai'.

Just another place to score

The London market is neither as established nor as violent as that of New York. 'Business' throughout the system, as in other spheres of production, appears to be conducted in a more amateurish fashion. This may be changing. There were indications by late 1980 that some freelance 'entrepreneurs of violence' (or thugs) were attempting to penetrate the distribution system at wholesale level in order to extort monopoly advantage from customers and importer/distributors unfamiliar with its structure. (Some Pakistani importers, for instance, took a little time at the turn of the decade to assess the extent of demand and adjust prices accordingly.)

In its essentials, the London distribution system conforms to Moore's New York-based model of 'vertical disintegration'. It is hybrid in the sense that it is neither truly competitive nor completely monopolistic. Relatively concentrated at import level, it becomes increasingly dispersed as the product flows downwards through a series of sub-levels. At each level there is a mark-up between buying and selling price, representing expenses, time expended, labour costs, overheads, relative risk in relation to arrest, theft or fraud, as well as a return on capital. Security considerations ensure that distribution units at each level are small, comparatively isolated and restricted in access.

Moore and Rottenberg[15] emphasize calculated risk as a primary factor in the generation of heroin profits, although, ironically, it is the consumer who runs a greater risk of both apprehension and harm due to the vulnerability of his/her position, the frequency of transactions undertaken and the toxic potential of the purchase. Illegality and risk are the ostensible reasons for secrecy, the restriction of access to supply, and the exclusion of consumers from all but the lowest levels of distribution. Such conditions can lead to substantial profits.

At retail level, profits are dispersed across a broad band of dealers and dealer/users, while at import level they are likely to be concentrated in the hands of relatively few individuals. The dispersed and fragmentary nature of the retail heroin market is such that it is unlikely that any single group or cartel could ever dominate the domestic delivery system from top to bottom. In terms of security and continuity of operation, the less bulk distributors/importers have to do with on the retail market the better are their chances of survival.

Given the bias of the market in favour of the supplier and the return on capital accrued at import level, the risks, on balance, are not enormous. Professional criminals, at least, seem to be drawing that conclusion. The extraction of surplus value from primary producers and secondary technicians in source countries, the market advantages for suppliers that come with illegality (of which risk is a major factor), and the popularity and demand for the drug itself are all primary components that contribute to the formation of price and profit on the British and international heroin market.

Depending upon their extent and duration, changes in price may indicate shifts in supply and demand that in turn stem from fundamental alterations in production, distribution and consumption within the overall global heroin economy. The sheer amount of heroin seized by HM Customs and Excise and the police between 1980 and 1983, compared to previous years, confirmed a major increase in production and delivery capacity in Southwest Asia, particularly Pakistan.[16] The seizure of such unprecedented quantities illustrates the ability of Customs to intercept large consignments at point of entry. However, there are no indications that these seizures created a significant reduction in overall supply. The quantities intercepted were an unknown proportion of the total amount of heroin delivered to Britain. It seems likely that seizures did not make a significant dent in the market. As things stand, source-country production capacity, the resilience of the illicit distribution system and an established and apparently growing demand suggest that the market will continue to flourish.

2. THE COST OF LACOSTE – DRUGS, STYLE AND MONEY

Lee O'Bryan

Ducking and diving

'Yeah, I don't mind a blow now and then, just to help me relax, oh yeah, sometimes a toot o' sulph . . .'

'Do me a favour, not even a baby could get off on that – you gotta 'ave at least a quarter of that to get a buzz'

Despite the sun and warmth of the summer day, we're sitting inside the drop-in centre for the unemployed. It's a grey prefab incongruously stuck alongside a once-thriving four-storey Victorian-built school. Thanks to the growth of new towns, like Basildon, taking many inner-city people away from their origins, there are now a number of similar empty shells in inner London. Part of this one is a sixth-form college specializing in business studies. This choice of specialization and the trickle of smart purposeful students is a bizarre contrast to the prefab and its world, where local unemployed kids can play pool and table tennis, make their own coffee and lunch and exercise at least some control over the day.

My companions this afternoon, an unusual trio of two punks and one casual – 'he's the only one who can play the drums' – are taking a break from discussing the lyrics of Mr Priest, one of a number of songs written in the quiet of a bedroom. Neil, one of the punks, and the main musical force in this small band discusses his gramme-a-day speed habit. He has recently given it the push, although the receding pricks along his inner arm show just how recently: 'We were going down the West End a lot having a laugh, getting into sulph, but it started to get too much, I started gettin' really paranoid, so I jacked it in, it was doing my head in'.

We're all agreed there's plenty of sulph, smack and black hash about, particularly from the squats and short-life housing blocks just a few hundred yards away, blocks well known locally as housing drug dealers. Jackie, a Scottish girl of about 22, stands by and casually folds a two-inch wad of notes: 'Well, I used to do about a gramme of sulph a day, and sell it, but I don't any more, it's a fucking mad scene'. She ambles off, and the musical trio get back to Mr Priest, laughing about playing to huge audiences at Wembley arena, living with the trappings of fame. Rehearsing every Thursday in the basement of an old church, guitars turned up full and shaking the snares and door frames, they are unaware of the wasteland between writing songs at home and fame, of negotiating with the music business – mid-Atlantic men idolizing the over-sanitized ethos of American FM radio. Take pity on us idealists who thought punk had blown away these gatekeepers of musical taste. They kept their heads down for a bit, but didn't take their hands off the throat of the music business for one minute.

But why think of that, it's only depressing. Like spending all your time worrying about finding a job which isn't there. At least the music provides a promised tunnel of light, something around which you can hang your days.

In some ways, this move to music is similar to the old

tradition of working-class boys taking to the ring to escape the poverty of slum areas like the Gorbals or the East End. Renowned as hard boys, boxers from these areas had the promise of good money as professionals. At the top end of the fight game money is still to be had, but lower down the scale the sport is in crisis. Non-title fights attract far smaller audiences than, say, 25 years ago, and there is increasing medical pressure to have the sport banned.

Just as snooker halls above Burton Tailor shops are a thing of the past, boxing gyms above pubs are increasingly difficult to find. The gym behind the 'Load of Hay' in north London is typical. Once used by ex-world champion John Conteh and scores of other young hopefuls, it has now been converted to a pink, green and white aerobics studio. At the best of times boxing was a longshot, now few young men can consider taking to the ring as a viable response to recession.

However, the musical response is not common amongst working-class kids today. For a start, punk, probably the most accessible (low-tech, easy to play) music for working-class young people has had its day. The few remaining punks have become highly politicized, involved in Stop The City demonstrations, covering Barclays Bank vending machines with superglue. The Rock Against Racism campaign of the mid- to late 1970s involved many working-class kids in an overtly political stance. No such campaigns are grabbing the imagination of young people today. A small number of mainly black kids are forming professional breakdance crews, but for most involvement is largely as a spectator or paying punter at a club.

So, if young working-class people aren't turning to

music or sports as they may have in the past, how are they responding to recession?

1985 – Spend now pay later time
'Not so long ago, style was something dodgy the continentals did. We in Britain had more solid Saxon values like hard work and thrift. Then there was inflation which made thrift a valueless virtue, and unemployment which made work a redundant aspiration.' (R. Elms, *The Face*)

Yes, it's jamboree time folks, spend now pay later time. Elms has described young working-class people from recession-bound areas such as the estates of Hackney and Islington wearing expensive designer-label clothes, using sophisticated and exotic drinks and drugs, driving flash cars and spending BIG MONEY. All the visible indices that prove the good life are there all right. In short, they're embracing the recession with conspicuously wide consuming arms.

But who exactly is Elms describing? Gary Kemp, of chart-topping Spandau Ballet, who drives a Porsche to escape the bleak realities of the oh-so-proletarian Escort XR3 may well be held to be typical. But let's face it, he's got to be loaded. The areas Elms describes are areas of massive gentrification – the wine bar and stripped-pine brigade. Has he mistakenly interpreted this influence as representing the working-class response? No, I don't think he has. The facelifted pubs complete with black matt paint contrasting with this season's greens and pinks, the showy cocktails and gathered curtains are clearly a relative of heavy-flock wallpaper, chandeliers in the hall of your council flat, and eighteenth-century reproduction television cabinets – the respectable working-class idea of style. Integral to the gentrification process is the idea of understatement, the stripped wood and vaguely 'country kitchens' altogether more reminiscent of an idealized village life of the past, which is a long way from the showy upfrontness of the new style and clubs.

Indeed, there's no denying that the fashion for designer clothes has percolated well into the large estates. Just as amongst the skins, where only a limited number and combination of clothes were acceptable, like Doctor Martens and Levi red tags, or sta-press and leather smooths, so only a limited number of designer-label clothes are given the seal of approval by working-class casual posers – with Nike, Lacoste and Toshini being amongst the most eminently respectable. There's no denying that those smart labelled jeans and colourful canvas trousers . . . those clean Nike trainers with thick coloured laces and socks look, well . . . bright. The stallholder down Brick Lane shouting, 'Sweatshirts here, right label, right price,' is reflecting the popularity of label clothes, and also the need to pick the right one. The pile of unsold goods is testament to the fact that he had the wrong label.

Perhaps the difference is one of just how conspicuous you can make your style look. Most need the frequent £5 bung from mum just to keep a limited wardrobe.

Central it may be, but it isn't enough wholly to explain the genesis of a style by simply relating it to the prevailing economic climate as Elms does. Styles do have a certain momentum of their own, the roots of this style clearly stretching back to the soul boys of the 1970s, of David Bowie's 'Young Americans'. But he has put his finger on why the style seems to be so widely popular now, particularly amongst working-class kids. It is some sort of attempt to banish recession.

Drugs, style and recession

The tabloids in 1984 took to their hearts the issue of youthful drug use like few others in recent years. Heroin addiction, numerous papers and occasional TV programmes have told us, is where working-class kids are really at today. The coverage of this issue has involved such hysterical and often inaccurate flag waving. Nevertheless, there is an issue here; the first half of the 1980s will be remembered as the period when drugs, including heroin, came to be used by increasing numbers of young people.

The tabloids have tended to place the responsibility for this at the feet of the individual. This attitude is shared by the government, which is hardly surprising considering their energetic contribution to the recession. For many others, however, the coincidence of recession and increased drug use are directly related, with such use being seen as an attempt to deaden the pain of unemployment.

In some ways, these accounts, stressing a degree of retreat and rejection of mainstream society, are similar to accounts of the hippies' drug use. One study, which contrasted hippies and bikers,[2] described hippy drug use as a means of spiritually escaping the constraints of straight society. Cannabis and hallucinogens were the most widely used drugs, heroin use regarded as the final and unalterable closure of relations with this straight society. A vague idea that Eastern cultures embodied non-materialistic values resulted in an adoption of Eastern dress such as kaftans and sandals.

In the film *Performance*, the implied inevitability of the East End gangster's adoption of hippy style whilst on his first 'trip' strikingly illustrates the supposed fit between drugs and this style.

But nobody wants to be a hippy these days, particularly not working-class kids. In its heyday, the hippy style appealed largely to middle-class people. Let's face it, even the gangster in *Performance* had to wear a wig on his trip, there wasn't really a place for him in the style. As an eminently employable group in boom times, young middle-class people could afford to drop out of the rat race, secure in the knowledge that re-entry would be a relatively painless operation.

For working-class kids then, and almost everyone now, there just isn't the room to get involved in such marginal styles and philosophies. With the government forcing you onto the scrap heap, the last thing you need is a philosophy which further marginalizes you. The appeal of the casual poser style is in its order; order that is being denied by the current economic policies. There is a paradox here, however, for the very government which has robbed so many people of their right to full membership of society won the last election with a whacking majority. Loads of young working-class people support the Tories, the party of order. This makes some sense if one accepts that the present government has managed to present itself as the embodiment of stability and solidness, albeit with a fair bit of help from Saatchi and Saatchi.

The widespread unpopularity of the hippies today means that an important source of wisdom and common definitions of drug experiences are no longer accessible to many young people. Without any youth culture to back up the notion that heroin is the 'big one', it becomes relatively easy, particularly for working-class kids who historically have always distanced themselves from hippy lore, to overcome the stigma of the stereotyped junkie. They can view heroin use not as a symbolic rejection of society but rather as something which frightens most people, holding a fair amount of status for those 'brave' enough to try it.

For a start, far less extreme ways of using smack are becoming increasingly popular. You don't have to inject heroin to get a hit. You don't get addicted on your first exposure to heroin, and while continuous sniffing or smoking can still lead to dependence, compared to injecting, it doesn't feel addictive, it's clean, easy. You can use it occasionally, keep clean and have a nice trouble-free time. In fact, after your first use, particularly if you don't inject it, you'll probably wonder what all the fuss was about, since it was really pleasant and not at all sordid.

This change in context is reflected in the absence of an identifiable drug culture amongst many estate kids who are using. If you're strung out on smack you'll probably wear jumpers during the summer to stop you from 'clucking' and long-sleeved shirts to hide the tell-tale needle marks. But these don't constitute the basis of a drug lore or style. Empty biro tubes used to inhale the smoke when 'chasing' smack don't look like becoming a fashion item. You can find users with non-using friends hanging about together and doing similar things with their time, often wearing similar mainstream casual clothes. Perhaps this change is best illustrated by the fashion of snorting heroin on the terraces of a north London football club a few seasons ago.

There are real dangers in adopting the hippy definitions in interpreting drug use today, a danger to which youth workers and other professionals in the area, many of whom grew up with these definitions, are particularly prone. This automatically defines an attitude to heroin use as being a response to problems, a retreatist exercise.

In fact, ideas of retreat and rejection sit uneasily with the group situations in which much use occurs, with the often intermittent patterns of use amongst young people, and with the upwardly mobile casual poser style.

This is not to say that everything is looking rosy. On many large estates where young people are using drugs things are looking pretty bleak. But was it ever fun to live on a large estate? This doesn't mean that young people's drug use is necessarily a retreat from all this.

The young people on these estates aren't angry, just trying to get by. If it comes along, you'll try some black, some sulph or smack, or perhaps something else. Yeh, there's some status to be had in trying that all right. Not glue though, kids do that, you can't stay cool if you're doing glue. 'What do you think I am, a wally or something?'

Don't imagine some people aren't having problems with heroin. Almost undoubtedly, any wave of occasional use is going to leave behind a higher number of people strung out than there were before.

'Here, pass us the vera's will you.' Ian proceeds to roll a joint of black. 'Well, I been doing nanoo nah for abaht nine months, a couple of us are tryin' to get off it, but I'm drinkin' like a fish, and doin' a lotta blow.'

A 20-year old white cockney, Ian has incorporated slang into his description of drugs. Hence vera (Lynn) rhymes with skin (cigarette papers). The origins of nanoo for heroin are unclear, but possibly originate from Greek dealers, dominant in one part of London.

'Of course, any person strung aht on nanoo wants to get off it'. Ian didn't start using heroin in order to get addicted. It felt nice, and he went overboard, and started using a lot of the stuff. His habit just sort of crept up on him. He wasn't feeling particularly depressed when he started using, and didn't really know how he got so into it. Some of his friends also got into a bad way, although his best friend and inspiration for his abstinence attempts hardly ever used. For many of his friends, occasional involvement is as far as it goes.

Why do some people develop such regular habits? Quite possibly, some people do have addictive personalities. Perhaps some do use drugs to deaden the pain of life or a particularly upsetting episode. Perhaps the absence of the hippy information culture means that people aren't necessarily aware that heroin can be addictive.

Drugs and money

Discussion of regular use raises the question of money. If your style is costing you, then how about drugs? Again taking a cue from the tabloids, drug addiction, aside from wrecking the individual, presents a major threat to the safety of property and people. For if you take drugs, you'll do anything to get your next fix. This is a controversial issue, and perhaps understandably so. Nevertheless, as is so often the case, if you do take your cue from the tabloids on this one, you're likely to end up with a pretty distorted picture.

Certainly, illegal money is to be made in the distribution structure, whether as a dealer or a runner. Not all drug users are involved in distribution networks, and anyway, it isn't this so much as drug users' potential involvement in other sorts of crime such as burglary and mugging to get drug money that seems to be causing the media and other social commentators so much concern.

With regard to this sort of criminal revenue raising

there is no clear-cut cause and effect relationship. For a start, much conventional wisdom fails to take into account the 16-year old who regularly steals a few pounds from his dad's wallet for the slot machines, and occasionally for a bit of black. Some people who go shoplifting for drugs money were shoplifting before to get other things, maybe food or just for spending money. Can you hold drugs responsible for this?

Similarly, regular heroin addicts have varying support structures which could well influence the response if skint and 'clucking'. Like Ian or Neil, you might try to give up, get some cheap drink, or ask a friend or agency for help. Alternatively, like one of Ian's friends, you might go and snatch a handbag – though a lot of good that did him, as he got caught and is doing six months at Her Majesty's pleasure for his pains.

The experience of Hoxton, a very traditional white working-class area in East London illustrates some of the fears and realities of the relationship between drugs and money. It is an area with well-established patterns of traditional criminality, typically burglary, but with an alleged morality of its own. In the old days, people will tell you, things were fine, nobody nicked in the area, they went elsewhere for the richer pickings of the nobs who had something worth nicking. These days there are a number of heavyweight drug dealers in the area, a high level of heroin use and an increase in local crime. Heroin is to blame say some locals, dividing the community, mutual self help smashed by people burgling in order to raise money for drugs.

But don't forget, in the old days, there wasn't anything worth nicking in Hoxton. Thanks to the magic of cheap rentals and the never-never, almost everyone has got a colour telly and a music centre, eminently moveable goods in the market for nicked gear.

In fact, those who remember a crime-free past are being romantic. Have they forgotten the local gas meter thieves nicking not for drug money but for a variety of reasons, maybe for drink, pocket money, anything? Likewise today, not all local crime is for drug money. But it is undeniable that there is more crime today, and unlike the gas meter thieves, who were universally condemned, local criminality is regarded as acceptable by growing numbers. This is even more depressing than the divisive effects of heroin. For the only real strength of the working-class community, looking after your own kind, cannot endure beyond the death of the extended family, and is breaking down in the face of material temptation – it's kick bollock and bite like anywhere else.

This has implications for the heroin supply structure. There is an idea amongst many sociologists that 'yer' traditional criminal loves his or her family, the 'Royals' (particularly the Queen and her mum), and generally is just too moral to move drugs. This doesn't take into account the effects of financial reward. Drugs are a good earner and as such are being invested with a pretty high status in the status league of crime.

If pressed to answer the debate on the causal relationship between heroin use and crime, the best answer, in a great sociological tradition is well, yes, no, and sometimes.

Few people can claim to be unaffected by the economic recession and I am in no doubt that for many there is a strong link between unemployment and drug use. But much work which stresses this link tends to suggest an oversimplified cause and effect relationship and at heart views drug use as a retreatist exercise. Undoubtedly the drug use of some could be described in such terms, but as a wider account such ideas sit uneasily with the drug market structure, the active entrepreneurial drug-selling talents of some users and the suggestions from my own fieldwork that opinion leaders in a group are often the first to try drugs. Certainly work along these simplistic causal lines cannot account for the drug use of people in secure employment or for decisions not to use by substantial numbers of the long-term unemployed.

To an increasing number of people, users and non-users, heroin no longer represents a symbolic gesture of rejection, and the special place and definitions afforded it in traditional hippy lore and literature has become less relevant. This has implications for people starting to use and for those using regularly, for in the absence of a binding core of accessible common wisdom it may be easier to use for the first time, and for some, unaware of the addictive nature of the drug, to use heavily and have problems of dependence.

But having said this, and after recognizing the significance of styles and the cultures behind them as sources of information, one should make it clear that only a minority of young people are getting involved with drugs today, and an even smaller number are experiencing difficulties. They may not have very much to be happy about, but things haven't fallen apart yet. Who was it who said 'the kids are alright'? They still are . . . just.

3. LOVE SEEDS AND CASH CROPS: THE CANNABIS COMMODITY MARKET

Tim Malyon

Hippy past, bullish present

Cannabis is an international commodity, like tea, coffee, sugar or oil. The money it generates wields immense financial, political and military power. Second largest cash crop in the US, largest cash crop in Jamaica, the Lebanon and a host of developing nations, its cultivation, harvesting, marketing and prohibition can feed or starve farmers, finance armies, buy businesses and control governments. Unlike tea, coffee, sugar or oil, this all happens without a vote being cast, tax paid, a word in business reports or serious mention in the press.

Twenty years ago, a writer on the left might have welcomed such a situation. Dealers were the new age Robin Hoods. In the US, the Brotherhood of Eternal Love, a huge, amorphous yet very real dealing organization was grossing millions of dollars from its cannabis and LSD operations. Much of this money filtered through into left wing and hippie politics; to activist groups such as the Weathermen, rock festivals and the antiwar movement. Countless businesses sprang up throughout Europe and the US promoting 'alternative' products like health foods and human awareness programmes, founded on seed capital from cannabis dealing. A host of radical bookshops, publishers and underground newspapers likewise came into being. The original source of all this revenue and optimistic activity, small farmers in Mexico, Pakistan, the Lebanon, became rich beyond their wildest dreams. Nobody suffered. The trade was 'righteous'.

This picture is an idealized one in some respects: the 'Robin Hoods' of the Brotherhood of Eternal Love were using Hell's Angels to distribute a sizeable slice of the product from the early 1960s onwards; and after the 1961 'Bay of Pigs' fiasco, expatriate rightwing Cubans with organized crime connections became involved in the trade, initially to raise money for Castro's overthrow. Nevertheless, much of the cannabis trade financed the cannabis message, 'peace and love'. For a few short years, the potent combination of revolutionary change and profitable underground business was a reality.

Today's scenario is different. In the Lebanon, approximately $1 billion per annum earned from the cannabis trade funds arms purchases, death and destruction. In the UK, 'dope [cannabis] dealing is seen as a sensible career alternative to armed robbery'. With certain exceptions, the international cannabis business is an unregulated commodity market where muscle, political and military connections, and ties with 'reputable' financial institutions to launder money are at a premium.

Narcs and the Narco-dollar

Foreign exchange earnings and employment in many developing nations are dependent on cannabis income. The cannabis 'narco-dollar' in Jamaica, for instance, contributes more (approximately $1 billion) to the island's foreign exchange earnings than all other exports combined ($710 million), including bauxite, sugar and tourism. Dollars paid for cannabis are used in turn to pay for fuel, food and other essential import items. Prime Minister Edward Seaga of Jamaica, a Harvard Business School graduate, stressed this point after his 1980 election. 'The ganja [cannabis] trade in the last several months was virtually keeping the economy alive,' he commented. 'It supplied black market dollars which were then used by industrialists and other persons in the economy who wanted to import raw materials for which they could not get Bank of Jamaica dollars. On that basis they were able to avert a lot of closures and substantial lay-offs.'

In any country, therefore, where cannabis earnings play an important role in the economy – Afghanistan, the Bahamas, Belize, Colombia, Egypt, Honduras, India, Jamaica, the Lebanon, Morocco, Nepal, Nigeria, Pakistan, the Philippines, Senegal, Sri Lanka, Swaziland, Thailand, to name but a few – two groups are able to exert considerable covert political, sometimes even military pressure. They are the exporters and growers and the various law enforcement agencies. The latter frequently derive massive covert income from pay-offs, sometimes earning more through such illicit channels than is paid to them by the state. These two pressure groups constitute veritable monopolies in some countries; in others are made up of independent factions. In either case, they are crucial powerbrokers, the more so because they operate with almost no public supervision or awareness.

Silent subversion

The US dominates international drug control policies, and is responsible, more than any other nation, for perpetuating the myth that domestic drug problems are largely caused by producer nations. US analysts locate supposed problems outside the domestic arena, rather than taking an honest look at the various levels of recreational drug use in contemporary US society. The United States is the single largest cannabis-consuming nation in the world.

For fiscal year 1985, the US is allocating $50.2 million to its own international narcotics control efforts, independent of the UN. The entire UN drug control budget for 1983, the most recent year for which figures are available, amounted to $6.8 million, the largest proportion of which was provided by the US.

Much of the US international drug enforcement budget is devoted to maintaining Drug Enforcement Administration (DEA) agents abroad. These officers are in a unique position to control a stream of information and disinformation to the press, tailored to US international foreign policy requirements. DEA news releases, on trafficking and use, are often reproduced verbatim by newspapers as 'fact', largely because of extraordinary ignorance about the politics of drug prohibition and lack of first-hand knowledge about what is happening within the drug trade. The situation is analogous to accepting all CIA reports on Allende's overthrow in Chile as historical fact.

From an official standpoint, DEA officers are representatives of a friendly foreign power, assisting the host government in controlling its drug problem. Under the United Nations Single Convention, signatory countries, in effect the majority of UN members, pledge to eradicate illicit drug use and trade, cannabis being a prime target. It was this treaty which forced Nepal to ban its most lucrative business, the trade in hashish, and which is demanding that Bangladesh eradicate all legal cannabis cultivation by 1989.

Signatory countries are therefore placed under an

obligation to eradicate what is often a vital sector of their economies. The US and UN may make pious statements about crop substitution, but no licit crop can begin to replace incomes from illicit cannabis cultivation. DEA agents, under instruction from US government officials, can pressurize specific governments into taking measures which lead to economic and political suicide: for example, cutting off the most important foreign currency earner and alienating large sectors of their populace.

The United States is threatening effective action against governments which do not toe the prohibitionist line. The US Congressional Select Committee on Narcotics Abuse and Control, dominated by the 'if it gets you high, ban it' school, is threatening both economic and military intervention against nations which fail to take sufficient measures to halt the illicit traffic. This crusading zeal reflects US foreign policy objectives, so that countries which do not comply will be selectively targeted for intervention. The result of this alliance of crusading zeal with political guile is the conversion of drug prohibition into an instrument of US foreign policy. Crop eradication programmes are used to destabilize certain nations, while in countries compliant with US foreign policy such programmes can serve as fronts for covert military intervention against insurgent sectors of the population.

Concerning military intervention, the Congressional Select Committee commented in its 1984 report that 'while insurgency is universally recognized as an internal political matter, it ceases to be completely so when the insurgents are a major factor in the international illicit narcotics trade.'[1] The US already supplies aircraft and arms to friendly states for crop eradication purposes. Only a small shift in emphasis is required to utilize such military hardware primarily for strikes against subversive areas. The Philippine and Sri Lankan governments have both, for instance, stated in recent UN Commission on Narcotic Drugs reports[2] that insurgents in their countries are using cannabis cultivation to generate funds for armed revolt. In the Philippines, the numbers of plants detected doubled to 1.8 million between 1982–3, whilst Sri Lankan herbal cannabis seizures rose from 11.5 to 70.5 tonnes during the same period. Central American states are also reporting increased cannabis cultivation: Guatemala seized 3 tonnes of plants in 1983, Honduras 20.9 tonnes. Allegations are increasingly appearing in the US press charging that guerrilla movements in these states, as well as the Nicaraguan government, are using the cannabis trade to boost their finances. Such claims, often supported by the DEA, are hard either to deny or substantiate. For a US administration seeking ways of supporting rightwing regimes, their publication is extremely convenient.

The ambiguous grey area between military aid and drug interdiction is further confused by the chemicals used in airborne crop spraying programmes to eradicate illicit cannabis cultivation. The most commonly used chemicals are paraquat, employed as a defoliant during the Vietnam war; glyphosate, better known by its trade name of 'round-up', a weed-killer capable of destroying a broad range of crops; and most recently, diesel oil emulsion. Aerial spraying of such substances, a somewhat random operation at the best of times, can have a devastating effect on food crops, water sources, marijuana, and people, be they drug cultivators or insurgents.

The rationale of current US cannabis prohibition policies is revealed in Wayne Greenhaw's *Flying High*[3].

Greenhaw investigated the activities of an international marijuana and cocaine trafficker, who claims that he paid the Somoza regime in Nicaragua $13.5 million over a ten-year period before the revolution. This was to facilitate unimpeded landing facilities for aircraft flying marijuana and cocaine from South America to the US. After the revolution, the trafficker moved his operations to Guatemala. He claims that similar arrangements exist with the Honduran, Salvadoran and Costa Rican governments.

Greenhaw also interviewed a former CIA agent who had worked in Central America. The agent confirms the allegations, then adds his own significant comment:

> Even the super-conservative guerrillas in Nicaragua –
> fighting against the Sandinista government that
> overthrew Somoza – have cut airstrips in jungle areas
> and they have allowed dope planes to land, refuel and
> take off. The CIA itself has helped in the construction
> of some of these strips with the knowledge that the
> planes from Colombia, bound for Texas or
> California, will be landing there.

While with one hand the US government suppresses the illegal traffic from some areas, if possible under a putative banner of fighting 'communist narcoterrorism', with the other hand it tolerates, even encourages, the illicit traffic in areas where it wishes ample funding to be available to anti-leftist terrorist groups, such as the Contras.

Neighbouring Belize is another case in point. In late 1983, the US Foreign Assistance Act was amended to require 'the suspension of assistance for failure to progressively eliminate the illicit production of narcotic crops'. Similar action is required under the Caribbean

Basin Initiative (CBI). And so Belize must face US prohibition wrath. With Nicaragua, Belize is the only Central American country to remain outside the US sphere of influence. Former Prime Minster George Price is an old friend of Michael Manley, and a former friend of the late Maurice Bishop. He has consistently refused US requests to station troops. Instead Belize relies on its garrison of British soldiers and aircraft to defend it.

The Reagan administration fears an independent Belize outside its sphere of influence, a possible haven for leftwing guerrillas and politicians fleeing Guatemala, Honduras or El Salvador. The cannabis pretext is therefore being used to destabilize the country and nudge it towards closer US involvement.

Belize has exported cannabis to the US and other markets for many years. Recent slumps in the world sugar market have made farmers more dependent on marijuana for their income. Thirty-two tons of cannabis were seized in 1982. A 1983 cannabis spraying programme in Belize wiped out large acreages of foodstuffs, such as beans, and proved so unpopular that it contributed to Prime Minister Price's loss of the 1984 election to his rival, Manuel Esquivel.

A spate of US-inspired publicity has placed this tiny nation in the limelight. President Reagan's special assistant on drug abuse, Dr Carlton Turner, visited in March 1985. Threats have been made to cut off US aid by the Select Committee on Narcotics Abuse and Control and also by the State Department, which pointed out that Belize receives 'more American aid per capita than most other countries'. DEA marijuana production figures of 3,500 tonnes per annum make Belize the fourth largest exporter to the US, after Colombia, Mexico and Jamaica. If this figure is true, the value of Belize's marijuana crop is approximately $350 million, as compared to total licit exports of $93.7 million.

While it is the case that American marijuana importers have been visiting Belize in recent years and have taught locals to grow sinsemilla-type cannabis, which fetches higher prices on the US market, the Belizean marijuana scare seems excessive. Belize must either initiate extensive crop spraying and eradication programmes, which will cause ecological turmoil, great suffering and widespread unrest, or aid will be cut, which will also cause widespread unrest. What the US is seeking is Belizean compliance with its Central American foreign policy objectives. The 'war on drugs' is a pretext to achieve this compliance. The recent arrest in Miami of Eligio Briceño, former Belizean Minister of Energy and Communication, on a charge of conspiring to export 5,000 lbs of marijuana per month to the US, has only served to increase the pressure. Briceño arranged the deal with DEA agents.

Nations under the British sphere of influence seem to have become favoured targets for high-level DEA entrapment exercises. In March 1985, Norman Saunders, at the time Prime Minister of the Turks and Caicos Islands, was arrested on charges of accepting massive bribes, offered by the DEA, to allow marijuana and cocaine traffickers to use the islands as transit points from South America to the US. At the time of writing he has resigned his post and is awaiting trial, with Stafford Missick, his Minister for Commerce and Development. They are both on $2 million bail. The British governor of the Turks and Caicos, Christopher Turner, issued a statement after the arrest saying that 'Mr Saunders is a highly regarded colleague with whom I had worked closely, not least in this government's efforts to curb drug trafficking in these islands,' but was then forced to admit that the DEA operation had his 'formal agreement'. The arrest may be connected with US attempts to negotiate relaxations in Turks and Caicos banking secrecy laws. Some banks of this off shore haven are used to wash trafficking funds, as well as supporting conventional tax avoidance schemes.

The world's largest cannabis producer?

It has been a consistent tenet of marijuana prohibition both in Europe and the US that the 'problem' originates with producer countries. 'Eradication [of illegal drug production] is the responsibility of the illegal producers; demand and use is created and sustained by their production, it is not the other way round.'[1] The rhetoric of cannabis prohibition demands that small developing nations cut off a crucial income source, and also in many cases their national, often sacred intoxicant, in order to solve the West's cannabis 'problem'. The hypocrisy of this position is astounding. The industrialized West hard-sells booze, tobacco and even pharmaceutical drugs already banned domestically to those same areas which it demands cut off their cannabis exports. The United States government, and the DEA in particular, are thus acutely embarrassed by recent revelations that its domestic marijuana production is booming.

As cannabis cultivation is illegal, exact figures are hard to calculate. The DEA estimate, however, that only 10 per cent of all cannabis consumed in the US is grown domestically, is politically rather than statistically inspired. The US cannot be seen to be producing a significant percentage of its crop domestically, otherwise its entire foreign prohibition and eradication policy would be exposed.

The US Select Committee on Narcotics Abuse and Control itself concedes that 4,000 tons of marijuana were cultivated in the US in 1984, up from 700 tons in 1980. A California committee of law enforcement and forest service experts has explicitly stated that 'Californians are concerned that marijuana is surpassing the nation's top cash crops . . .' In Hawaii a similar committee reported that 'marijuana is surpassing pineapples as Hawaii's number-one cash crop'. NORML, the US National Organization for the Reform of Marijuana Laws, is a cannabis legalization lobby which has over its 15-year existence established a reputation for cautious reliability. Based on reports from all its state organizations, it estimates that '55 per cent of marijuana consumed in the US was grown domestically . . . Marijuana is ranked as one of the top three cash crops in 22 states, and is the number-one crop in 10 states.'[4] It estimates the total value of the 1984 US domestic cannabis crop at $16.6 billion, second to corn ($20.4 billion) but surpassing soybeans ($11.9 billion). Even if the low DEA estimates are accepted, cannabis is still a more valuable crop in the US than tobacco.

Furthermore, domestic cultivation is booming. The 1984 crop is estimated by NORML to have been 20 per cent larger than the 1983 one, with increased emphasis now being placed on indoor cultivation. In US terms, indoor cultivation is not simply a few plants in a small attic. Massive barns and warehouses are used with sophisticated hydroponic systems. Ed Rosenthal's latest book, *Marijuana Grower's Handbook: Indoor Greenhouse Edition* has sold 4,000 copies in prepublication sales while *Sinsemilla Tips*, a journal for marijuana growers with a circulation of over 6,000, is starting its fifth year of publication.

The US law enforcement response to domestic cultivation provides a rare insight into what peasant farmers in other producing nations are already experiencing. The DEA has organized a nationwide marijuana eradication programme, named CAMP (Campaign Against Marijuana Planting).

In California, this programme has been stopped by District Court Judge Robert Aguilar because of civil liberty injunctions. The following sworn report was one of many similar stories which contributed to his 1984 decision:

> CAMP troops blocked Judy Rolicheck's driveway with a vehicle on August 16. The troops called for her and the other residents to 'come out with their hands up'. When they complied, they found the house surrounded by 15 troops, with their guns drawn, dressed in camouflage clothing and sheriff's uniforms. The Rolicheck's family dog ran up barking. Ms Rolicheck asked if she could tie up the dog so it wouldn't be in the way and was told 'No'. Instead, the troops shot and killed the dog.'[5]

The troops had no search warrant, her house was searched for two and a half hours, nothing illegal was found, and no-one was arrested. Judge Aguilar compared the CAMP operations to Orwell's *1984* after troops had occupied the entire town of Denny, California.

If such paramilitary terror tactics are being used in California, with all its media coverage and safeguards against civil liberty breaches, then it's a sure bet that more than dogs are being shot in developing nations where no such safeguards are available. Whole regions of marijuana cultivation are brought under military control, as happened in Colombia in 1979–80, when 12,000 troops occupied the Guajira peninsula. During 1984, 1,500 hectares of cannabis cultivations were destroyed manually in Colombia, while 3,000 hectares were sprayed with the defoliant round-up.

The US domestic marijuana eradication programme, CAMP, has caused widespread anger in many areas, both from growers and others not involved in the trade. Opposition has been kindled by high-handed police tactics and local awareness that in many rural areas cannabis cultivation has profited more people than just the growers. Cultivation has brought widespread prosperity where before there was stagnation and depression. The following is a typical comment by a small-time but successful grower in Northern California:

> With luck, you'll survive, bring in your harvest, reap
> the rewards of a long season both in good smoke and
> bucks. And you'll probably spend a bunch of that
> money in the local hardware and grocery stores,
> maybe buy that long-promised rototiller from the
> feed store and a bunch of lumber from the building
> supply for the new shed. Since you can't bank what's
> left over, and it won't do anybody any good in a hole
> in the ground, you might loan some to a neighbour
> who needs it to build a house, or maybe to the food
> co-op that's buying a new building . . . marijuana
> growers will make the difference between continuing
> rural economic stagnation and prosperity.

This comment highlights the idealistic aspect of marijuana cultivation. In recent years, increased violence, including shootings and booby-trapped plantations, have been associated with cultivation. Growers now find willing banks to launder their money. However, the basic scenario of economic revival created by marijuana cultivation still holds true, for California, and even more so for countries like Belize, Colombia, Jamaica, the Lebanon, India and a host of others. David Burrows, Youth Officer in the Bahamian Ministry of Youth, Sports and Community Affairs, commented recently: 'For the first time, the rural areas have money and are doing well. To ask the people to give up is difficult.'

Bibles in the ganja fields

'A cultivation with about 5,000 growing ganja trees and a nursery, containing about 2,000 seedlings was found in the hills of Longville . . . and destroyed by a party of police . . . An open Bible, showing the 27th Psalm, and held down by two stones, was found in the field on the ground. No arrest was made.' (*Jamaican Star*)

The path climbed steeply, spiralling up toward Blue Mountain Peak, at 7,402 ft Jamaica's summit. Tiny terraced fields clung to the slope, irrigated by streams and intricate piping systems constructed from the ubiquitous bamboo. It felt fine to be out, pacing the mountain, away from the oppressive heat of downtown Kingston. Up here, small ganja plantations are crucial to the peasant farming economy; they represent the difference between bankruptcy and a viable smallholding. By a wooden shack in the last village below the peak stood a young Rastaman, blowing smoke into the still evening air. An inquisitive smile lit his face and silently he fell in beside me, passing the large 'spliff'. Thus we trod easily up through the village, burning herbs without a word.

Above the village we rested, squatting on the crest of the hill where I dropped the backpack. My new companion was a local ganja farmer. Swiftly he disappeared, only to return with 'a whole heap o' herb' wrapped in brown paper. Tearing strips off the paper, he proceeded to roll up cigar-sized 'spliffs'.

Born in the country, my companion, Leon, had followed the example of many youthful friends in the 1960s and moved to Kingston. Unable, like a third of the population, to find a job, he had returned. His Rasta faith, with its stress on clean eating and being grounded in the natural environment, had encouraged him in this. Now the ganja income assisted him in building up his smallholding and achieving a measure of self-sufficiency from the 'Babylonian shitstem' on which he had turned his back. 'Not car, buy two goat', was the reply made by another Rasta farmer when asked what he did with the profit from his crop.

Approximately 70 per cent of the Jamaican rural population use marijuana in some form, either smoking it or drinking it as a medicinal tea. Many workers on the sugar cane plantations smoke it, believing that their strength and ability to endure the gruelling work are thereby enhanced. Until the early 1960s, cultivation of the plant was for domestic use on the island. Then, with the arrival of Western 'hippy' tourists, in particular Americans, the plant's economic potential as an export crop started to be realized. When the oil price hikes in the early 1970s threw Jamaica's economy into crisis, ganja plugged part of the gap in foreign exchange earnings.

Shortly after my encounter with Leon, I visited another

cannabis plantation which graphically illustrated the influence of the foreign market on domestic cultivation. Three farmers were cultivating alongside one another, one old man and two youths. They shared duty watching the plants as harvest time approached, sleeping in a hut erected from wood and palm leaves. The oldest farmer was still cultivating traditional 'kali weed', seeded cannabis, harvesting as soon as seed started to form on the female plant buds. His young neighbours, however, under the advice of US importers, were growing 'sinsemilla', pulling up male plants as soon as their sex could be distinguished, allowing the unfertilized females to keep on growing, producing ever larger and more valuable buds in their desire to attract male pollen. When I arrived, the youths were attempting to persuade the old man to do the same, so that their female plants would not be fertilized by his males. He remained sceptical, suspicious that this might be another sophisticated yankee plot to eradicate cultivation by ridding farmers of their seed stocks. I visited the fields with a small-time US importer, a man who was making a comfortable living from the trade, dealing directly with several growers throughout the island.

According to official US government estimates, Jamaica is the third largest supplier of cannabis to the US, after Colombia and Mexico. It is estimated to export between 2,000 and 4,500 tonnes to the US. Canada is another massive market. A recent confidential report from the UK Central Drugs Intelligence Unit stated that Jamaica is 'the most frequently encountered source country for herbal cannabis' entering Britain. Cannabis is the island's largest cash crop, with a value equivalent to one-third of the total legal gross national product. Not only is it the largest cash crop; it is also the only business, with the possible exception of music, which is booming.

The significance of ganja in Jamaica is not simply a matter of the massive financial worth of the crop. It is as much a question of who controls that money, and what cultural significance the plant possesses on the island.

Over 90 per cent of Jamaica's population is black, mainly descendants of African slaves shipped by the British to work the colonial sugar plantations. Also shipped in by the British were indentured labourers from India, whose descendants form 3 per cent of the present population. Africans and Indians are the two largest ethnic groups. The island's indigenous Arawak Indian population was long ago destroyed by force, famine and disease.

These origins provide the key to ganja's social and political significance in Jamaica. For many Indians and Africans, ganja, not alcohol, is the traditional recreational drug, a herb which in both societies is imbued with great spiritual significance. In India, cannabis is the sacrament of the deity Kali, the plant which breaks down the constraints of rational mind. Similar spiritual beliefs are held in many African societies. A recent study by Brian du Toit[6] has shown that in South Africa cannabis remains a vital symbol in preserving cultural integrity. One old man commented to him: 'Cannabis was the smoke of our ancestors. It was smoked by all the great men who were fierce fighters and wise in deliberation. And since it is the smoke of our fathers, it is said, we must smoke it too.'

It is not by chance, therefore, that ganja has been adopted as a holy sacrament and symbol of African roots by Rastafarians; and also by West Indian youths, in Jamaica and abroad, rebelling against accepted values of

Western white society. One popular Jamaican rhyme inverts the usual image of alcohol as the 'successful' intoxicant, ganja as the backward, rural, 'lazy' drug.

> You drink white rum you tumble down
> You smoke kali weed, you succeed.

Many reggae songs in Jamaica link ganja-smoking with freedom from 'downpression', including several by the late Bob Marley and Peter Tosh. Dr Freddy Hickling, former Senior Medical Officer at Kingston's Bellevue Psychiatric Hospital said in 1980: 'The reality of ganja is related to its rebelliousness, its restiveness among the native populations of colonized countries; the fact that people use this and will disobey the ruling dictates of the time.'

Ganja's association with Rastafarians connects it with an ideological stance which is opposed to a takeover of Jamaican culture by American business and Western commodity values. Dr Horace Campbell from the Institute of Development Studies, Sussex, has characterized 'the cultural resistance of Rasta' as 'an integral part of the struggle against American imperialism and commodity fetishism, which attempts to reduce human beings to zombies'. One example of this was the part played by Rastas in the Grenadan revolution: 'In Grenada, the brethren have shown that with ideology and organization they can be mobilized to participate in a revolution. More than 400 Rastas were involved in the People's Liberation Army of the New Jewel Movement which overthrew the Eric Gairy dictatorship.' Rastas were later disillusioned by the NJM when the extreme Left of the movement started to characterize growers on the island as right-wing infiltrators. The original example remains however: Rasta and its ideological fellow travellers are potent revolutionary forces in Caribbean politics, and perpetuate ganja's symbolic value as a herb of protest.

The trend in the Jamaican ganja export busines is one of increasing centralization. The difference between $40 per lb obtainable on the domestic market and approximately $120 per lb obtainable from exports puts anyone with bulk transport out of the island in a key position. It has led to the present situation where small exporters and their farmer customers are being increasingly squeezed. The bulk exporters, who have resources and contacts to pay big bribe money, are taking over an ever-larger slice of the market. Small farmers and dealers, already hard pressed by the dire state of the Jamaican economy, are the losers. Major exporters can dictate prices 'at the field' and also indirectly expose their competitors to law enforcement harassment. This trend was beginning in 1980 and by all accounts is increasing. One message is coming out very clearly from the island: law enforcement operations, intended partly to appease the US, partly to cut out competition, are hitting the small operators and leaving major movers alone: Dawn Rich, writing in the *Jamaican Daily Gleaner* in the early 1980s, stated, 'Jamaican small farmers are in the process of being recolonized by an extremely dubious Miami outfit which proposes to use an indigenous cult – Rastafarianism – as its religious cover, so that it can be free to market ganja . . . in the United States.' One striking example of an alleged major marijuana exporter from Jamaica, and US importer, is the Ethiopian Zion Coptic Church, a religious sect with many beliefs similar to Rastafari. Unlike Rasta, however, the Coptic Church is effectively controlled by white people. The organization is also highly centralized, immensely wealthy and viewed with grave distruct by many Rastas. The Coptic Church (no connection with Ethiopian Orthodox Coptics) is virulently opposed to Michael Manley's PNP, which is referred to as 'the Communists'. It is significant, in view of ganja's symbolic importance, that the Coptic Church is at the same time a spiritual 'competitor' to Rasta, anti-leftist, and, supposedly, a major force in the Jamaican ganja trade.

The Coptic Church has immense influence within Jamaica. On the island, the Church owns over 4,000 acres of farmland and a supermarket stocked with its own produce. This immense food production capacity gives the Coptics considerable leverage, leaving aside all their other business interests. In 1980, it operated the largest container transport business on the island, handling both government and private contracts between Jamaica and the US. It owned a furniture business and was the island's major automobile importer, handling British Leyland, Toyota, Datsun, GMC and Volkswagen. Since then, its legitimate business interests have expanded. When I visited the Church in 1980, Manley's government was still in power. The IMF had withdrawn all funding and credit and the island was desperately short of foreign exchange. This was not the situation with the Coptic Church and its businesses, however.

By 1980, over 1,000 people were on the Church payroll in Jamaica. In the US, it owned a huge mansion on Star Island, Miami, for which $270,000 was paid, cash, and a Florida farm, from which ten tons of marijuana was seized. US Customs were claiming duty of $15.5 million on a further 1980 seizure.

Several of the Church's leading American members are now serving sentences in the United States on various cannabis importation, trafficking and conspiracy charges, involving two specific importations amounting to 33 $\frac{1}{2}$ tons, and 'unloading multi-ton quantities of marijuana on six separate occasions.' They were also charged with 'the bribing of Jamaican military officers to obtain information as to the location and planning of the Jamaican Coast Guard and Defence Force.'

I spoke with a Coptic member on Star Island, Miami, in 1985. It is most striking that his account of ganja law enforcement in Jamaica directly contradicts all other accounts I have heard concerning recent police pressure: 'The Seaga government hasn't really persecuted us at all in Jamaica,' he stated. 'The government's attitude is that ganja is better than Communism. If it fights ganja too hard, then people will become antagonistic and turn to Communism, that's the other party, Michael Manley's party. So they prefer to allow the ganja to grow.'

Jamaican Prime Minister Edward Seaga is a shrewd businessman and politician. One of his first actions after beating Michael Manley at the polls in 1980 was directed towards Jamaica's bankers, acknowledging publicly the crucial role played by ganja dollars in keeping the island's economy afloat, and requesting banks to 'take foreign money from clients without asking too many questions.' Despite such remarks and because of his vital role in Caribbean politics, he has avoided US prohibitionist wrath. He supported the US invasion of Grenada and unlike his rival, Michael Manley, he is virulently opposed to the Castro regime in Cuba. Seaga is, however, in deep domestic political trouble at present. Following a 20 per cent increase in fuel prices in January 1985, thousands of Jamaicans took to the streets in protest. At least seven people died during two days of violent clashes with security forces. Any real pressure by the United States to cut off aid or make serious moves against cannabis traffickers would bring down his government, which is currently trailing the PNP in the opinion polls. Seaga knows this. So, he is in a position to 'play the cannabis card'.

Shortly after his election in 1980, while negotiating with the United States for a major aid package, Seaga gave an interview on ganja and its role in the Jamaican economy. He played off the ganja trade, and US disapproval of this, against the sure knowledge that the US needed him in its fight against Caribbean Communism. 'The question of legalizing it,' he stated, 'so as to bring the flow of the several hundred million dollars in this parallel market through the official channels and therefore have it count as part of our foreign exchange – which would mean an extremely big boost to our foreign exchange earnings – is not just an economic one. It is a moral one and requires a lot of study.' For Seaga, the moral question is not one of medical harm – 'medical reports seem to suggest there's no conclusive evidence that ganja is harmful' – but rather of corruption. 'There is a moral problem . . . that is the bribery that runs with illicit traffic. And in at least two cases, we know of gun trafficking that has been associated with it.'

'Regardless of whether we want it or not,' Seaga continued, 'the industry as such is here to stay. It is just not possible for it to be wiped out, and if it is here to stay then we have to make up our mind from that point as to how best to deal with it.'

Seaga was asked directly whether he was linking the cannabis traffic with a major US aid package. 'We have not brought together these things as a quid pro quo, and I would hope to avoid that,' he said carefully. 'But I believe that if you're going to analyse Jamaica's problems at any depth at all at this stage, you are going to run into the fact that this huge traffic is going on – which you may not consider to be to the advantage of your country [i.e. the USA] – and you are going to raise that question, and I in turn am going to have to say, well, it's keeping us alive. How else do we get kept alive?'

This comment is as close as any politician can come to saying directly, 'Give us generous aid, or we will legalize it.' A US embassy official in Kingston commented drily after the interview: 'Seaga is walking a tightrope. When the planes fall out of the sky, they will have to go out and arrest people. But that's about it.' In other words, no major traffickers will be arrested unless absolutely necessary.

The point was graphically illustrated to me while I was photographing an illegal landing strip in Jamaica. I was approached by a major in the Jamaican Defence Force who believed me to be a trafficker, a common problem when investigating the trade. He informed me that use of the airstrip would cost 5,000 Jamaican dollars, at that time about £1,000.

'We may have goofed . . .'
Between 8 and 11 November 1984, some 10,000 tonnes of marijuana were seized near the US/Mexican border in the Mexican state of Chihuahua. This single seizure amounted to eight times the official DEA estimates for marijuana production in Mexico. 'We may have goofed,' commented a DEA agent. The DEA were particularly embarrassed by the size of this seizure because Mexico had been held up as a model country in drug eradication. It has co-operated in marijuana and opium crop-spraying programmes, even

assisted in the Belizean crop-spraying venture. Through the 1960s, Mexico supplied the US with 95 per cent of its imported marijuana, this figure dropping to about 5 per cent after pressure had been brought to bear on Mexico, and Colombian production had come 'on stream'. Recently, Mexican production has been rising once again, considerably faster than the DEA realized.

Then early in 1985 a DEA agent was kidnapped in Mexico. His body was found in March. Intense pressure was put on the Mexican government by the US to 'do something'. The government's action caused yet more embarrassment. Two supposedly leading figures in the Mexican trade were arrested. One has allegedly confessed to ownership of the 10,000 tonnes. Both claim that they controlled at least 800 police through bribery.

If the allegations are true, what emerges from this incident is another example of centralization in the cannabis trade, centralization which through police corruption poses a threat to democratic government. The trade effectively creates a state within a state. This does not benefit the peasant growers. According to J.P. Gené, writing in *Libération* in early 1985[7], 7,000 local people were hired to work on the farms growing this marijuana. They were initially promised $15 per day, and then forced to work for a plate of red beans a day in conditions he describes as 'akin to *The Grapes of Wrath*'. So long as cannabis remains illegal, and thus effectively an unregulated commodity market, such situations will arise. This is the lesson of the 10,000 tonnes in Mexico, a lesson which is doubtless being repeated in many areas around the world at this moment.

Dope for guns
It has become something of a tired cliché in international narcotics reports that the illicit drugs business is intimately linked with international terrorism and the arms trade. Many sectors of national and international cannabis markets have indeed become linked with arms dealing and armed insurrection. It would be astonishing were this not the case. Money knows no politics, save that the Right usually seems to end up with more of it than the Left.

The Lebanon is a prime example. From 1976 onwards, Lebanese hashish started to flood European, British and US markets. It is still much in evidence. Harvests produced a minimum of 10,000 tonnes annually, a maximum, according to some observers, of 100,000 tonnes. Official cannabis seizures in 1981 amounted to 446 kilos, a remarkably low figure which illustrates the extent of corruption more than it does the size of the trade. Control of the Lebanese cannabis trade extends into the highest echelons of Lebanese financial and political power.

Taking the lowest estimate, the harvest was worth approximately $1 billion 'on the beach' for export, $30 billion on the streets of Europe and the United States. Lebanon's 1982 official gross domestic product was $1.68 billion, its official exports $645.5 million.

The main growing areas are in the Upper Bekaa and Hermil Hills to the North. Eighty per cent of the cultivated land in this region is estimated to be devoted to marijuana plantations, whereas before the 1975-6 outbreak of hostilities, the figure was only 10 per cent. There are also large areas of cultivation to the east, near the Syrian border. Fields are now protected by tanks and armed guards. Producing areas had by 1981 assumed an air of prosperity, with good roads, expensive cars and well-maintained houses and hospitals.

Although these production areas are Moslem dominated, much of the distribution chain is controlled by Christians. Both PLO and Phalangists have profited from the crop, with trafficking routes running into Israel and Egypt, and from Lebanon's sea ports to Europe and the US. The US has complained that 'frequent allegations of Syrian government tolerance of the hashish production and traffic in Lebanese territory under its control are reported.' Syria does indeed effectively control the main production areas, and can exert considerable leverage over funding for various covert organizations through this state of affairs.

Another region where hashish and arms trading have become inextricably linked is Southwest Asia, specifically the tribal territories bordering Afghanistan and Pakistan. Pakistan has now surpassed the Lebanon as the primary supplier of hashish to the USA. In Europe, the last two years have seen a resurgence of 'black' hashish, mainly of Pakistani or Afghani origin. An April 1985 seizure in Pakistan of 17.5 tonnes of hashish indicates that the trade is flourishing.

Most hashish-producing regions lie in territories only nominally under the control of either the Pakistani or Afghani governments. The war in Afghanistan has lead to higher levels of arms dealing and further slackening of control. As one Pakistan government official commented to the BBC recently: 'Before the war in Afghanistan, the tribes had single-shot rifles and a few automatics smuggled in at great cost. These days, it's a woebegone sub-tribe that doesn't have machine guns, mortars, even anti-aircraft guns. It is no longer easy to exert control over them.'

Ever since the British and Russians vied for political supremacy in this region during the nineteenth century, the tribes have played off superior powers against each other, often 'serving' both powers simultaneously. A recent Pakistan government effort to crack down on the heroin trade in one tribal area demonstrated how volatile the situation is. According to the BBC, the tribal leader switched allegiance to the Soviets as a result of Pakistan's actions.

Publicity concerning illicit drug production in the region has focused on heroin. According to informed visitors to the region, many erstwhile cannabis middlemen supplying the US and European markets have now moved entirely into heroin dealing. Profits are larger, transport and detection less problematic. Some middlemen are content to supply both commodities. Such is the demand for foreign currency to purchase arms, so tenuous is central government control of the region, that all illicit drug markets have been experiencing ideal boom conditions.

Drugs have become a crucial financial and political issue in the area. Pakistan is under increasing Western pressure to cut back on heroin production. The UK government has even dispatched 'our man in Karachi' to solve the problem. Western government and UN reports have significantly neglected, however, to make prominent mention of the cannabis trade. There may be a reason for this. According to Alex Brodie, BBC correspondent in Islamabad, 'the heroin trade can only be stopped with the agreement of the tribes. If that were forthcoming, the pressure might have to be taken off hashish and opium. If the chiefs ban heroin, the government might have to back off on other issues. But it will have to be done by negotiation, because, as a Pakistani official put it: "To disarm the tribes these days, you'd need the Pakistani, the Afghan and the Russian armies." '

In this region, as in Central America, the CIA and drug enforcement officials are in effect working against each other. The CIA wishes to maximize Mujahideen war efforts against the Russians in Afghanistan. This includes assistance in weapons procurement, mainly through Pakistani military channels. The Mujahideen are however undersupplied with armaments, as recent Western news reports have indicated. Unless the US increases military aid, the only other real source for arms funding is the drugs trade, hashish, heroin and opium.

It thus seems possible that an increasingly blind eye will be turned to hashish production, in return for reductions in heroin trafficking. This is the only effective way of solving the political and military impasse outlined above; and it seriously weakens international cannabis prohibition.

Cannabis in Britain

Approximately 500 tonnes of cannabis are consumed in Britain every year (see Appendix, p. 103). Street sales are worth some $1.5 billion. If all cannabis dealers and wholesalers were to be amalgamated into a single mono-polistic concern, it would rank amongst the *Financial Times* top ten UK companies in turnover and profitability.

No such monopoly exists. The cannabis market is extremely diverse, encompassing thousands of small dealers and importers, as well as a number of larger companies. The size of seizures over recent years suggests that several organizations are regularly importing amounts between $2\frac{1}{2}$-5 tonnes. Uniformity of price in different areas of the country, as well as frequent availability of one type of cannabis over the space of several months in different regions indicates that multi-ton quantities are dominating the market. A 1980 importation of 15 tons of Colombian marijuana, however, proved difficult for the wholesalers to shift sufficiently swiftly. This may have been because the British market is primarily a hash market, but does indicate that an importation of this size is somewhat impractical, exposing importers to all the risks inherent in long-term storage.

As well as bulk quantities of uniform cannabis types, most frequently Lebanese and Pakistani hashish, and increasingly herbal cannabis of indeterminate origins, a large variety of different types of cannabis is available on the market in smaller quantities. Especially during the winter months leading up to Christmas such 'specials' appear, usually of exceptional quality. The cannabis market is, in this respect, somewhat similar to the wine market, with cheaper wholesale brands and lines for the connoisseur.

The existence of the latter indicates that a considerable number of '1960s-style' dealers are still plying their trade. Such importers possess cherished personal contacts with small growers and producers in prime-quality production areas. They buy by the kilo rather than in ton quantities, immediately after the harvest when the product is at its most fresh. Their overhead costs, and risks, are high in comparison to larger importers, since they must export from producer countries and import into the UK using their wits rather than bribe money. From the viewpoint of producer farmers, however, such traders represent a better return on their product than large exporters. They usually buy direct from farmers and because of this will pay a better price for good quality. This quality is what allows them to recoup costs. An ounce of high-quality black hashish would retail in the UK at around £120, rather more than the £80-£90 paid for medium-quality gear.

Northern India is a classic producing area for such small-time traders, although this situation is now rapidly changing. In the autumn in the lush valleys which characterize the southern slopes of the Himalayas, farmers can be seen rubbing both wild and cultivated plants between their hands, producing little sausages of prime-quality hashish. Piles of such sausages are weighed out on old-fashioned scales in the villages and sold directly to traders who have walked up into these remote, beautiful areas.

Here, hashish is as good a currency as conventional cash. The farmers are smallholder peasants, often very poor, cannabis their main cash crop. This income tides them over bad years when the harvest fails and they must purchase food. In recent times, deforestation has caused devastating floods, landslides and loss of agricultural land. For some farmers, the hash harvest, and a contact with a Western dealer, has been the lifeline which has tided them over such catastrophes. For many of these people, hashish is both cash and their sacred herb.

From robbers to dealers

In Britain, traditional criminals have been encroaching on the cannabis market. During the middle and late 1970s, a whole generation of robbers were forced to change their trade, largely as a result of 'supergrass' trials which put many operators behind bars. The process is still continuing. These men, in their forties, were also wary of a new generation of thieves hitting the streets, 'heavy characters, wound-up speed freaks, pilled up to their eyebrows on the job and likely to kill somebody', as one informant told me.

Having been rendered redundant in the robbery business, they were in search of a new trade. For many, free retraining was copped at Her Majesty's pleasure. They met up with cannabis smugglers also serving time, and old taboos against 'druggies' were gradually broken down: 'Former vodka and martini brigaders were introduced to cannabis for the first time in prison, and loved it. They bought it off screws, or girlfriends would bring it in. Some extraordinary kissing was taking place at the end of visiting time.' Warders would often turn a blind eye and some became involved in the trade. 'Warders would rather prisoners were sitting in their cells out of their skulls than causing trouble.' Eventually, cannabis, cocaine, and to a lesser extent heroin, became prison currency.

Inevitably many ex-cons entered the dealing business when they came out, sometimes in partnership with traditional dealers they had met in jail. The trade was less risky than major robbery, weapons less evident, jobs required less planning, and a regular turnover with reasonable profits could be confidently expected.

The other advantage enjoyed by former robbers entering the trade was that they frequently possessed considerable sums of money for investment earned from previous jobs. In a trade where 'front' money is a valuable asset, considerably increasing profit margins, this assured them of rapid success. The late 1970s and early 1980s saw a popular 'scam' involving gold bullion smuggled from abroad. Bullion purchased abroad without VAT payment would be smuggled into Britain, sold and the VAT pocketed. Proceeds, once this scheme was rumbled, were often funnelled into the cannabis business.

The movement of conventional criminals into drugs also coincided with an increasing acceptability of cannabis and cocaine, as well as heroin, amongst the 'chic' rich. Contacts established in clubland, illegal drinking establishments and the entertainment industry could be easily exploited for marketing drugs. And working-class leisure venues, such as pubs, were providing semi-public areas for sales. A ready-made circle of trusted colleagues was also available, willing to become involved in the leg-work of dealing – transport, warehousing, money-laundering.

A classic example of working-class criminals becoming involved in the illicit drugs trade is that of some notorious members of the Dunne family of Dublin. During the late 1970s and early 1980s, they graduated from robbery to dominating the growing Dublin heroin market. Their activities were not, however, confined to heroin. They also dealt in large quantities of cannabis, especially in the period before heroin reached epidemic levels in the city.

Not all villains graduated to cannabis dealing late in life, however. I watched one informal network grow up in South London during the early and mid-1970s. All came from working-class backgrounds with no particular taboo against illegal trades. The area also contained a large number of middle-class dropouts and a ready market for a variety of mind-bending substances. This particular group were happy to put their hand to anything which earned the odd penny, be it selling 'blues' (speed), LSD or cannabis. Some were inclined to violence, others distinctly hippy in outlook yet disarmingly realistic about making money. They started out by moving the odd ounce, then brought back VW buses from Morocco, and finally, when

VW buses were too obvious, established connections for tonnage loads.

Contrary to popular misconception, commercial profits on cannabis dealing are not vast. Cannabis retailers stand to make profits of around £450 on an investment of £1,450 in 2 lbs of medium-quality hashish (January 1985 prices). It would take most dealers two weeks to sell such a quantity, affording a weekly income of £225 less at least £40 expenses. This income must be assessed in the context of treating dealers of all illicit substances as 'merchants of death' deserving stretches in jail of $3\frac{1}{2}$–14 years.

In times of unemployment, dealing is a career option for many people. As an alternative to the dole queue, dealing still tempts desperate importing strategies, such as carrying large quantities of cannabis into Heathrow airport from producer countries neatly packed in suitcases. The relatively low mark-up on cannabis has also lead to the establishment of semi-public retail outlets with high volumes of trade. Such establishments, which exist in most major UK, European and US cities, are able to exist thanks to increasing social acceptability of use and police pay-offs.

Fifteen tons and what did he get?

'Not guilty.' A classic saga of the 1970s and 1980s involved the ubiquitous Denis Howard Marks, an Oxford graduate. Marks enjoys the distinction of having been caught with full accounts and computerized pay-in records of a 15-ton cannabis importation into Scotland from South America. He charmed his way out of the scam in front of an Old Bailey jury who liked him sufficiently to swallow a preposterous story and acquit him.

The Marks story is now well publicized, especially in

David Leigh's book, *High Time*,[8] which was written with considerable assistance from Marks himself. Marks smuggled only cannabis, made several millions from it, and organized remarkably eclectic importation and wholesaling teams, including an accountant, a barrister, several working-class friends from his schooldays, and an Irishman who has claimed to supply arms to the Provos.

The Marks story highlights the wide range of people involved in the cannabis trade. His methods, exposed by various witnesses during his trial, were also a classic example of expert money movement, which is becoming increasingly sophisticated and entrenched within 'respectable' financial institutions.

From New Year's Eve 1979, when 15 tons of Colombian cannabis were landed on a remote Scottish beach, to May 1980, when Marks was arrested, some three tons of cannabis were sold and paid for, grossing a little under £2 million. Marks' share was 10 per cent, the load having been 'fronted' by US investors. The cash pay-in system was computerized by James Goldsack, an old friend of Marks, accountant and son-in-law of a judge. Patrick Lane, Marks' brother-in-law, arranged the channels for exporting these huge sums of cash. The £2 million has never been traced beyond the initial stages of its movement overseas.

Patrick Lane set up a tax avoidance company registered in the Cayman Islands and functioning legally. He gained the trust of a respectable New York bank. Its New York president introduced Patrick Lane to the bank's British representatives. They were informed by Lane that he wished to transfer large sums of cash out of the country, the earnings of pop groups wishing to avoid tax, and money belonging to members of the Indian community who desired to conceal its export. The representatives testified s prosecution witnesses at Mark's trial that they had received $\frac{1}{2}$ — 1 per cent of the exported proceeds for their services.

Different company names and personal names were used on pay-in slips, some real, some false. Different banks were used to pay in the cash to avoid suspicion. These two tactics avoided one of the main problems in exporting illicit cannabis money: paying in huge amounts of cash to the banking system without arousing suspicion. The money was sent sometimes to Lane's account in New York, sometimes transferred to Hong Kong, sometimes sent to Zürich and Amsterdam. From these external accounts it was transferred once again, and lost in a maze of offshore companies and tax fronts. Old-fashioned in the sense that he only dealt cannabis, Marks thought modern in his money movements. Even the Inland Revenue, having demanded £$\frac{1}{4}$ million tax from Marks on his illicit activities, was forced to settle for much less. Patrick Lane has never been found.

Going to the cleaners
International money-laundering has now reached massive proportions. British businessman David Gould, until 1983 a senior executive of a leading firm of City accountants, was charged in the USA in early 1985 with 'conspiracy to violate US currency laws'. He was allegedly arranging to charter a plane to fly cash to the Bahamas from Atlantic City, New Jersey. The First National Bank of Boston was fined $\$\frac{1}{2}$ million in 1985 after pleading guilty to failing to report $1.22 billion cash transactions, 'some of the paper-bag variety'. Any payments in cash of over $10,000 must now be reported by US banks.

As these examples how, international money-laundering is now entrenched within the 'reputable' financial system. It is this particular aspect of trafficking organizations which law enforcement bodies are attempting most zealously to trace. However, there is little effective difference in the methods employed by legal corporations sending money abroad to avoid tax, and an illicit trafficking concern paying its profits into offshore banks and 'front' investment companies. Current attempts by the UN and domestic governments, therefore, to penetrate banking protection afforded to traffickers and increase seizure powers of funds are doomed to failure. To be truly successful, these initiatives would entail the exposure of many apparently reputable corporate operations, a development unacceptable to the international business community. If increased financial and property seizure powers are in fact granted to domestic law enforcement bodies, they will simply result in the confiscation of assets from small traffickers and increase the stranglehold of large organizations on the business.

A striking example of this was provided by the testimony of convicted trafficker, Harold Oldham, to the Permanent Subcommittee on Investigations of the US Senate Committee on Governmental Affairs in November 1981:

I might add that he [a Cayman Island financial advisor] stated that in his opinion and in his experience, virtually all the money transiting the Cayman Islands is doing so for tax evasion purposes. His clients were certainly not exclusively narcotics' people but also major entertainers, professional people, multinational companies, et cetera, and the

same he felt held true of clients of his fellow
Caymanian corporate representatives.

The weak spot, for traffickers and corporations alike,
in laundering funds is taking the cash or transferring the
funds to the tax haven. Once paid into the haven, they are
virtually untraceable. In this respect, the following
anecdote related by Oldham is highly significant, indicat-
ing just how impractical it is to tackle the political
hornets' nest of money-laundering.

At that time the primary access to the Caymans was
through Miami Airport and the flights to the
Caymans left out of gate number one. Gate number
one was the only gate at the Miami Airport – and to
my knowledge almost any airport in the United States
– that did not have metal-detecting devices or any
security of any kind. I cannot explain this. I only
know that at that time it was easy just to walk from
the ticket counter onto the aircraft without any
examination of any kind.

Wrapping it up
If an anthropologist working in the Amazonian jungle
had discovered cannabis being used by a previously
undiscovered tribe; if a multinational tobacco company
had been sold it as a new product to compensate for
sluggish tobacco sales; if it had been advertised on ITV
and sold in off-licenses, or advertised on Channel Four and
sold in health food shops as a new herbal tranquillizer –
would it have become as popular as it is now?
In US states where it has been decriminalized, use does
not appear to have increased. In Amsterdam, where

public sale in specific clubs and bars has long been tolerated, there are indications that use may even be declining somewhat. If all the resources of the drug prohibition establishment had been devoted to advertising and marketing the dread weed, would consumption be greater than it is now?

In the West, cannabis is becoming an increasingly acceptable intoxicant, its consumption and marketing spread amongst all classes and sectors of society. It is even regaining 'street cred', perhaps because of a hardening in some quarters of repressive attitudes to it. 'A filthy trade' is what one judge called its sale in March 1985 in Torquay, sentencing the vendor caught with $6\frac{1}{2}$ ozs to $3\frac{1}{2}$ years in jail.

Having openly advocated cannabis legalization for many years, the question in my mind is not, 'When will reason and humanity prevail', but rather, 'How much more can the system take before it is no longer worth its while to play this game?' Cannabis seizures rose worldwide by 57 per cent last year, not because of improved law enforcement, but because the business is getting bigger. In the US, the *Boston Business Journal* and *Wall Street Journal* have been discussing how much tax the federal government could make out of the trade if legalized – $5–10 billion per annum are the current estimates.

There is no sign of change amongst popular politicians, although some conservative columnists in the US, such as William Buckley and Sydney Harris are rocking the boat. Their grounds for change are not humanitarian, but practical. Sydney Harris wrote in the *Detroit Free Press*:

If I were asked what I thought was the greatest government scam perpetrated upon the American public, I would unhesitatingly name our so-called war on dope. It is a fraud on at least three counts: it cannot succeed, it will continue to suck billions out of the national treasury, and it will swell the ranks of bureaucratic enforcers and line the pockets of corrupt cops and politicians.

Some narcs are starting to complain: 'The law on possession [of cannabis] is fairly unenforceable and it points to a growing lack of conviction that it is a sensible law' (Tony Judge, UK Police Federation Spokesperson). 'If it was clear that the smoking [of cannabis] took place merely for the personal satisfaction of a few, you may decide to do nothing.' (Sir Kenneth Newman, in guidelines to the Metropolitan Police on what to do at a pot party). Police officers now openly disregard cannabis smoking and dealing at certain rock festivals and in 'areas with large West Indian populations' (*Police Review*) because otherwise they would have riots on their hands.

And corruption? According to the *Sunday Times*, a whole town in New South Wales, Australia, has been taken over by cannabis cultivators, police and all, with protection for their activities extending up to a former member of the federal cabinet. The dismissal of a former operational head of the London Drug Squad after 'recycled' cannabis had been seized for the second time, covered in fingerprint powder, seems small beer in comparison.

Jamaica could be the first country to make a move on legalization. In 1983, Jamaica's external debt consumed 41 per cent of all export earnings in interest payments and repayments. The debt now amounts to $3.2 billion and will for ever burden the island. Or will it? What if Michael

Manley won the next election and declared a moratorium on foreign debt? All IMF and US aid would probably be cut off. 'The question of legitimate marijuana exposes me to extreme temptation,' Manley said in 1978. 'As you know, Jamaica has a balance of payments crisis and we have never been able to get the marijuana sales to pass through our bank.' Shortly after he made that statement, the IMF cut off all funding to Jamaica because Manley would not accept their stringent monetarist strictures on his social programmes. He went to the polls in what was dubbed 'the IMF election', and lost. Also in 1978, Manley commented ruefully, 'I don't know. Someday somebody will jump into the breach and say, "It's legal now." Maybe it will have to be me.' What will he do the next time a government he leads faces draconian IMF demands?

If Manley did get marijuana sales to pass through the bank, would US marines invade next day? Or impose a total military blockade on the island? That would depend on prevailing domestic opinion in the US where a more liberal administration might start initiating a new wave of reforms similar to the decriminalization measures of the Johnson/Carter era. Perhaps other cannabis-producing nations would follow Manley's example – in strictly economic terms they could not afford not to do so. A new regime in Pakistan might also feel cannabis legalization to be the only way of pacifying the North-West Frontier and reducing heroin production which is having such dire domestic addiction results, incurring international odium.

Cannabis has been providing useful services to humanity for over 5,000 years. The Chinese were using it as a fibre and medicine before 2,000 BC; the Scythians were stoned in 500 BC and 'howling in joy'. Set against such a long history, the last half-century of prohibition pales into insignificance, an episode comparable in stupidity to US alcohol prohibition. Cannabis is, after all, just another plant, just another cash crop; unless we choose to make more of it.

Appendix: Cannabis Use in Britain
Mathew Atha and Sean Blanchard

Since 1982 the Legalize Cannabis Campaign (LCC) has sponsored two surveys into cannabis use. The first studied the basic use patterns of campaign members, the second looked at drug users at two rock festivals. While neither study claims to be fully representative of cannabis users as a whole, they provide the only statistical insights available into how cannabis is used in Britain.

The surveys used anonymous questionnaires. The first was distributed through LCC branches in autumn 1982, the second from LCC stalls at the Stonehenge and Glastonbury festivals in June 1984.

Both surveys sampled users throughout Britain. The average age was 25 for the members survey, 23 for the festivals survey. In both cases the age range was wide, with a broad peak between 18–30 years, and a long tail of older users, the oldest being a 67-year-old pensioner. Most occupations were represented, with many professional people, skilled workers, artists, students and businessmen. There was one former policeman.

Most users had been educated beyond school-leaving age, over half had a higher education. One in five had children, although only 8% were married. Approximately half were living alone, 40 per cent in a steady relationship, 5 per cent divorced or separated, and 1 per cent gay. A third lived in their own home, 60 per cent in rented accommodation, and 8 per cent were homeless or living in a squat.

The cannabis market

The price of cannabis seems remarkably stable throughout Britain, with Lebanese hashish the most popular variety (42 per cent of market) at £16 per ¼ oz, followed by black hashish from the Indian subcontinent (30 per cent market) at around £22 per ¼ oz. These markets appear highly organized with stable prices. Moroccan hashish (£14 per ½ oz) captures 10 per cent of the market, though prices vary considerably.

Only 9 per cent of cannabis consumed by festival goers is imported herbal cannabis, although the latter accounts for 36 per cent of cannabis seizures by police. This discrepancy can be explained by the preference for herbal cannabis by the black community (which was not adequately represented in these surveys) and the greater tendency for police to stop and search black youths, particularly in London where this practice has increased by over 60 per cent since the abolition of the 'sus' laws.

Around 9 per cent of cannabis consumed was home-grown, and three-quarters of participants had tried to grow cannabis plants. Two-thirds had sold cannabis, though the majority had done this at cost price to friends and acquaintances.

Consumption

Approximately two-thirds of cannabis is consumed in 'joints' mixed with tobacco. The average smoker consumed six joints per day shared between four people, thus representing an average daily consumption of 1½ joints a day. There is, however, wide variation in consumption figures, with a small number of users smoking up to 20 joints a day. Around 20 per cent of cannabis is smoked unadulterated, in pipes, 5 per cent (herbal cannabis) smoked in neat 'spliffs', around 5 per cent eaten, and the remainder consumed by such exotic methods as vaporization on red-hot knives.

About 60 per cent of both samples were daily cannabis users. This figure differs from the findings of other studies which have observed that only 20–30 per cent of all people who have ever used cannabis do so daily. However, many users have been smoking cannabis daily for over 15 years. In both LCC studies, the average user would purchase about $\frac{1}{2}$ oz of cannabis per month, although a small minority would consume over 2 ozs monthly.

Other drugs

Only the festival survey studied other drug usage. The most popular drugs used were LSD, 'magic' mushrooms and 'speed'. Of these three, the psychedelics were the most popular, although only a tiny minority used them regularly. Around 5 per cent of the festival sample used 'speed' at least weekly. Half had used cocaine, although only 1 per cent were regular users. Barbiturates were unpopular and very few people had inhaled solvents. The vast majority of respondents had not used heroin, most stating that they never intended to do so. Out of 614 completed surveys, only three people used heroin daily.

Drugs and the law

A small number of users wanted cannabis to remain illegal, claiming liberalization would 'take the fun out of it'. One in seven expressed no view. Over three-quarters of subjects expressed the desire for cannabis to be legalized or decriminalized. Only 9 per cent wanted all drugs freely available, and 7 per cent called for heavier penalties against 'hard' drugs.

Twenty-two per cent of the festival sample had been convicted of a drug offence, over 80 per cent of these for possession of cannabis. Those with a drug conviction, and homeless users, were more likely to have other convictions as well. Although three-quarters of the sample had no criminal record, over half had been searched by police for drugs.

Drug problems
4.8 per cent of the sample had received treatment for drug problems. All these were either heroin or amphetamine users. Of all those who had used heroin, approximately one-third had stopped without assistance.

How many cannabis users are there?
These surveys suggest that approximately 2 million people smoke cannabis daily in Britain. Furthermore, in 1979 the sales of hand-rolling tobacco were only sufficient to account for about two-thirds of Rizla cigarette papers sold. The shortfall would suffice to make 12,000 million joints, or roughly 3.5 million joints per day. With a daily user consuming 1.5 joints, this figure corresponds roughly to the survey estimate. Other recent surveys also support the 2 million daily users estimate, including one by Granada TV in January 1984, which found that 34 per cent of their sample admitted to using cannabis at least once. This would suggest, if repeated nationally, that over 10 million people had tried cannabis; approximately a quarter of these would be expected to become daily users. Based on these figures, the UK consumes about 500

tonnes of cannabis per annum, worth approximately £1.5 billion.

4. PSYCHOTROPICS, PASSIVITY AND THE PHARMACEUTICAL INDUSTRY

Betsy Ettore

Women, public health and economic decline

For Britain, the welfare state has brought an enhancement of human welfare and social values apparently more humane than those of the laissez-faire economy of previous years. This has been reflected in the growth of state responsibility for health, education and social security. By the late 1970s, these social services accounted for one half of all state expenditure.[1]

Since 1948, the state has financed an organized system of medical care, the National Health Service, based on the idea that direct investment in health care enhances 'national prosperity' or more specifically, 'public health'. Through the development of the NHS, 'wellbeing as a social right' has become established. The marriage between social welfare and public health under the umbrella of the NHS has an important social consequence: the right of each individual to his/her own wellbeing is seen to be managed and safeguarded by the state.

During the last 30 years, women's position as health care consumers has been affected by various social changes. Firstly, there has been a considerable rise in the number of married women in the labour force. In 1951, one in five married women had a job, by 1976 it was one in two. In 1981, two out of three employed women were married.[2] Secondly, social definitions of women have changed and it is more socially acceptable to define women as both workers and mothers. However, it has been suggested[3] that while definitions of femininity have been 'liberalized', there has been little change in society's view of women's identity as essentially domestic and subordinate, a view traditionally upheld in society and currently challenged today by women researchers.[4] Thirdly, in recent years unemployment amongst women has increased more than three times faster than that of men.[5]

During the current economic recession, these three changes put women into a vulnerable economic position and into a prime situation to become depressed, to be welfare consumers or to become involved in the drug world. Research has shown that medical-psychiatric symptoms in women are related to isolation in the home, stress produced by poverty and to lack of employment, as well as stressful life events.[6] Furthermore, women have a higher incidence of depression than men, their depression being rooted in unexpressed anger relating to their subservient social roles.

In a society supposedly based on social welfare, public health and individual wellbeing, the occurrence of depression, mental stress, anxiety or any other symptom which may lead to 'mental illness' is frowned upon. Yet, women's social position and the nature of the female role as it is constructed is conducive to mental illness. Women are the major consumers of health care within the British National Health Service. Furthermore, women are one and a half times as likely as men to enter a psychiatric hospital at some period in their lives.[7] In effect, women are categorized more often than men as 'depressed', 'psychoneurotic', 'psychotic' or as 'suffering from non-specific disorders'.[8]

As a select group of welfare consumers, women are more vulnerable than men to changes within the provision for social services. The welfare state is partly about making non-workers, such as unemployed housewives, participate in the economy by consuming the state's services. This type of participation is seen as an alternative to retreatism, an option which Offe views as involving dependence on 'subcultures, drugs or communes'.[9]

The prescription of psychotropic drugs within the NHS and with the support of the pharmaceutical industry may be one way the state allows women the option of retreatism, while still exhibiting control over this particular option (dependence on drugs). On the other hand, self-prescription of psychotropics whether they be obtained licitly (i.e. alcohol or NHS prescriptions) or illicitly (i.e. barbiturates, opioids, etc., from the 'black market') may be for some women a refusal to be be manipulated by the state in their choice of 'retreatism'. Whether or not drug use involves purchasing and consuming an illegal and/or a legal commodity, it has been suggested that international drug consumption has reached its highest level ever.[10] Furthermore, in the United States the illegal drug market has expanded during recent years to include drugs such as diazepam (Valium, Librium, etc.) which were previously available to users only through the medical profession. In this context it is important to mention that benzodiazepines are not included in any international convention on prohibition.

Comfort in the bottle: public health v. state profit
Let us look briefly at the structure of the alcohol market:

its effect on women who as a group have increased their consumption of alcohol in relation to men[11] and the economic benefit the state receives from alcohol consumption.

In Britain, consumers spend approximately between £7½ and £8 billion a year on alcohol. This represents 8 per cent of total consumer expenditure. The state makes approximately £2,500 million a year from taxes on alcohol.[12] There is a $170 billion global alcohol market, dominated by 27 major multinational corporations each of which have sales exceeding $1 billion a year and with branches in eight major industrialized nations.[13] Britain houses nine of these 27 corporations.

During the economic recession of the late 1970s, these British multinationals were forced to expand and create new markets both at home and abroad. Markets were sought abroad in the Third World, while at home market growth was generated through the development of alcohol sales in multiple retail chain stores, such as Marks & Spencer, Sainsburys, Tesco, Safeways and International Stores, a subsidiary of British American Tobacco. Alcohol became available at lower retail prices and by 1977 approximately half of Britain's supermarkets had licenses to sell alcohol.[14] One major consequence of this latter development has been that women are increasingly targeted as consumers by producers and retailers.

Regardless of what the state calls the costs of alcohol misuse (estimates range from £400 million to £650 million), it nevertheless makes a profit of at least £1,800 million a year from alcohol revenue. Officially, the treatment of alcoholics costs the NHS £8 million a year.[15] While state profit from alcohol consumption appears to take priority over public health, any persons suffering from individual problems related to alcohol consumption is labelled a 'misuser'. Women lost out not only by being prime targets for alcohol marketing strategies but also by being less likely than men to receive treatment if seeking 'comfort in a bottle' gets a little out of hand.[16]

Women as health-care consumers: an investment in passivity
In economic terms, one of the most significant penetrations of private capital into the NHS has been through the pharmaceutical industry. This is primarily multinational, with a small number of firms, such as Hoffman La Roche, dominating the world market. In this context, public health may have more to do with a 'healthy' pharmaceutical industry than has been previously considered.

Since information produced each year by the Prescription Pricing Authority (PPA) on what drugs are prescribed by the NHS (by brands, quantities and price) is kept secret by the DHSS, it is difficult to establish the exact relationship between the NHS and the pharmaceutical industry. We do know, however, that in 1949 and 1983 all NHS prescriptions numbered 225.1 million and 386.3 million respectively and that prescription numbers rose steadily over this period of 35 years.[17] We also know that in 1977 the NHS Drug Bill amounted to £596 million,[18] in 1981, £1,067.6 million, and in 1982, £1,233.2 million.[19]

In 1984, psychotropics represented 15 per cent of all prescriptions written by GPs[20] and 17 per cent of all NHS prescriptions. The Institute for the Study of Drug Dependence (ISDD) has collected information on a variety of local and national surveys on psychotropic drugs. One 1971 survey on tranquillizer/sedative use showed that 14 per cent of the adult population had used these drugs and that there were twice as many women as men, meaning that one in five women and one in ten men had taken these drugs in that year.[21] Another 1977 study suggested that 12 per cent of the adult population in England and Wales had taken a prescribed psychotropic drug in the previous fortnight and that 7 per cent had first been prescribed that drug a year or more ago.[22] MIND[23] states that thousands of people have been taking these drugs for up to 15 years and 1.5 per cent of the adult population have been taking them for a year or more. The national picture of psychotropic drug use is particularly grim for women. There is twice as much use of prescribed psychotropics by women as compared to men. The peak usage is found amongst middle-class, elderly women and is often long-term.

Between 1965–70 there was a 19 per cent increase in prescriptions for psychotropic drugs[24] and between 1961–71 it was 48 per cent. Also Lader[25] drew attention to the higher rate of use among women on both a national and international scale.

During the 1960s, doctors prescribed amphetamines as daytime antidepressants, while barbiturates were used for night-time sedation. Some of these drugs became popular on the illicit drug market and by the early 1970s policies were being aimed at those 'misusers' who obtained drugs on the black market.[26] Doctors themselves set up CURB (Campaign on the Use and Restriction of Barbiturates) in 1975 to help reduce the prescribing of barbiturates. While in the 1970s 'barb freaks' were unable to get tranquillizers to supplement their drug habits, housewives of the 1980s can easily obtain tranquilizers to supplement theirs.

Between 1970–75 the number of barbiturate and stimulant prescriptions decreased, while for tranquillizers and antidepressants the number went up.[27] Williams points out that prescribing statistics for psychotropics do not include drugs prescribed for out-patients and in-patients and therefore must be interpreted cautiously. Furthermore, benzodiazepines may be prescribed as tranquillizers, hypnotics or anti-convulsants and these prescriptions may be counted under different drug group headings.

Nevertheless, the changes in prescribing practices could suggest that doctors are increasingly prescribing drugs classed as antidepressants and tranquillizers for night-time sedation. Minor tranquillizers, such as benzodiazepines, were marketed as being effective both as daytime tranquillizers and night-time sedation. Benzodiazepines were believed to be more effective and safer than barbiturates in alleviating anxiety and stress, in dealing with 'the extent of clinical anxiety in society'.[28]

However, like barbiturates, benzodiazepines have been related to both psychological and physical dependence[29] and the Committee on the Review of Medicines reported in 1980[30] 'the lack of firm evidence of efficacy which might support the long-term use of benzodiazepines in insomnia and anxiety.' Recently, it was stated that the problem of dependence on tranquillizers is particularly relevant to women as they take these drugs and encounter dependence problems twice as much as men.[31]

With nearly 40 million benzodiazepine prescriptions at a cost of almost £30 million to the NHS and given the 'invisible' cost to the lives of thousands of women users, the use of benzodiazepines should be considered a social issue worthy of critical attention. The issue is about a growing NHS investment in the 'image' of women as 'passive consumers'. It is also about the aggressive marketing strategies of the pharmaceutical industry which, like the alcohol industry, targets women. For women, the result is the perpetuation of their passivity and domesticity.

Release, a national organization concerned with the problem of tranquillizers and how it relates to women, estimates that money invested by the pharmaceutical industry in advertising and promotion represents twice the amount spent on research and development.[32] Further-more, there is one drug company representative for every eight general practitioners in Britain. Melville[33] reported that out of 115 drug advertisements for tranquillizers in the *British Medical Journal*, 91 referred directly to women patients. Geared to women, the message of most psycho-tropic drug advertisements is that everyday stress is a medical problem. Intervention is oriented towards the individual who is under stress rather than towards a society in need of change.[34] Women have become a prime market for psychotropics; during a period of economic decline, society needs to keep its growing number of non-workers (women) in their traditional roles of house-wives, mothers, caretakers and nurturers.

The use of psychotropic drugs by women can be seen, like depression[35], as an 'escape' from the oppressive nature of the domestic role located within a subservient social sphere. In structurally powerless positions of wife/husband and patient/doctor,[36] women are trained to gain whatever comfort, joys or pleasures they can. The supply of psychotropics is allowed by the state, promoted by the pharmaceutical industry and 'demanded' by the female patient who asks, 'Doctor, can you give me something to make me feel better, less anxious and less depressed?' The hidden question is, 'Doctor, can you help me to feel less socially inferior?' Often, the answer to both questions is a pill.

The relationship between women and the medical

profession can be seen historically as a relationship of social control.[37] The consequence of this development is that women become more dependent than men on the institution of medicine, and the relationship between a woman using tranquillizers and her doctor may reveal a process of collusion. Within this process, a woman may be denied and may also deny an active role in maintaining her drug supply. On the other hand, long-term consumption may be consistent with a woman's own social expectation to 'follow her doctor's orders'. With the current move to put a restriction on supplies by the state, a media campaign well-symbolized by the book, and more recently the film, *I'm Dancing as Fast as I Can*, induces guilt and shame in women drug users. The pharmaceutical industry's response has been to promote more socially fashionable products, such as vitamins, which have high consumer acceptability.

The hierarchy of dependences: forbidden desires and social taboo

When the problems of women drug users are taken out of the private domain, society's experts often fail to see the reasons why women use. drugs differently from men. Women's drug use may be seen as more of a social problem than men's use because it implies 'de-stability' in the family. There are no public settings, contexts or mechanisms whereby women can address their experiences in terms of the choices they make or the benefits they receive from drug use. Underlying the invisibility of their drug use is the type of voluntary, active and creative use of drugs, which Harpwood describes and illustrates so well.[38]

As targets of both the greed of the drug industry and the

ignorance of the medical profession, women have emerged in their traditional role: passive consumers. Unless women become conscious of their need for pleasure and perhaps their need for more pleasure with or without drugs, their role as passive consumers will be perpetuated. A consideration of notions such as 'becoming an active consumer' or 'taking control of one's drug use' may be an appropriate beginning, if women users desire to challenge their current situation.

Within society, the use of both licit and illicit drugs involves a socially constructed hierarchy, ranging from 'good drugs' at the top of the hierarchy to 'bad drugs' at the bottom. On the hierarchy of addictions, tranquillizers are seen as 'good' and socially necessary to maintain domestic bliss or the stability of the family. It is interesting to note that there has been no research on tranquillizers which emphasizes the consumer viewpoint. This lack may exist because women appear to be the 'primary consumers'. Society's prescription that women are to be dependent overrides any experience that women, whether as individuals or as a group, have as independent beings.[39]

5. COCAINE FUTURES
Anthony Henman

1. Meet the Players: An Introduction

You are sitting in a street-side café in Cochabamba, Bolivia, waiting for that break which will really open up the cocaine business to serious scrutiny. Your contact – Guillermo, a member of the city's traditional land-owning elite – is laying down the bullshit, between calls for another round of *Taquiña* beer and the rattle of dice across the table-top: 'Lucho [a small-time cocaine manufacturer] has gone back to using ether . . . he says he prefers the buzz from the fumes. Acetone makes him sick.'

The journalist to whom these words are addressed, not wanting to seem ill-informed, takes up the challenge: 'The problem's not the acetone, but his drying techniques. Lucho's *merca* [from *mercancia*, or 'merchandise'] comes out too compacted. It's got too many lumps in it.'

So? A bearded sage, later to be identified as a sociologist, hears their words and springs to the defence of local industry: 'Give Lucho a break. It's good to see someone still using ether these days, what with all the pressure on supplies. As for the drying, it depends on whether he's got those 200-watt light bulbs installed yet.'

You wonder: how is it that these three characters all

know so much about one small and apparently insignificant cocaine lab? Could this be a deliberate send-up for your benefit? Across the table, an American with the glazed eyes of a remittance man from California listens in on the esoterica of cocaine manufacture with obvious interest. You suppose that anyone so laid-back would have to be here in the capacity of a user/buyer of some discrimination, anxious to pick up points of style that will lend him a certain status on returning home. But you notice also that the polite formality shown towards him by the local luminaries is tempered by not a little nervousness. Every American is not only a potential buyer. He is also a potential nark.

This doesn't, however, prevent him from chipping in: 'Hey, Guillermo, what about that pink flake you were on about yesterday? You reckon it's cooked up yet?' (Mythical overtones, here, as real pink flake is actually pretty rare – a holy grail for errant coke lovers.) 'Toot sweet, *sí señor*,' replies Guillermo, employing a little mock deference.

As he springs to his feet, you reflect on the social ironies underlying this brief exchange. Guillermo, the faded aristo with a strong suit in downward mobility ('our family estates were taken over by the peasants in the land reforms of the 1950s') can also lay on a bit of nationalist resentment as a sop to his less exalted countrymen. Together they can detest *yanquis* for their economic and political stranglehold over the continent, and righteously defend the cocaine industry as Bolivia's only way out of its current crisis. Equally, they can bad-mouth their major buyers for a brash philistinism and lack of grace matched only by the Brazilian *noveaux riches* – significantly, their number-two market, and poised perhaps to take the lead. Not least, they can take the piss out of all and sundry in a subtle way, providing confusing and contradictory accounts of cocaine prices and qualities, and laying deliberate red herrings in the path of potential narks and interlopers of any stripe.

After a brief absence, Guillermo returns, his features lit up with a big smile which says that he has scored: 'Not the pink, but something we connoisseurs prefer.' He proceeds with a detailed account of how flake cocaine – with its long, fish-scale crystalline structure – is actually a devil of a nuisance to chop up into the requisite fine dust. Indeed, on withdrawing to the privacy of the gents, you are soon poring over a dull, yellowish powder quite lacking in the glint and glitter which flash magazines would have you believe is the sign of the Real Thing. 'This cocaine,' pontificates Guillermo, 'has been intentionally *under*-refined, and then crystallized out with very great care, which requires the services of an expert chemist. The yellow tint shows that there are still impurities in it – other alkaloids like hygrine. This gives you a more rounded high.'

Thank you, Guillermo.

It is worth considering what lessons can be drawn from this type of encounter, repeated in countless cafés the length and breadth of South America. That the finer points of quality should attract so much obsessive attention from users and dealers is perhaps understand-able, but why is there such a lack of seriousness in examining the wider impact of the cocaine business on local societies? With a few – very few – honourable exceptions, media and scientific output on the question has noticeably failed to break any really new ground. Most accounts limit themselves to one or more of the following elements: pious rhetoric about the drug 'problem' backed up by questionable medical data; alarm at the evident corruption produced by the illicit traffic, combined with political sniping at rival interest groups; and, quite often, a liberal mixture of superficial anecdotal material ('How I failed to interview the great cocaine king . . .') designed to provide street credibility and the flavour of real involvement in the scene. Why is this formula so pervasive?

One explanation, suggested by James Dunkerley in a recent political history of Bolivia,[1] is that 'the world in which cocaine is fabricated, transported and marketed is obscure, resistant to intrusion and, as a consequence, prone to description that employs exaggerated hyperbole and the most grotesque conspiracy theories'. While not denying that hyperbole and conspiracy theories do exist aplenty, it could be argued that the root cause of this lies less in the opacity of the coke scene itself than in the intellectual vices of the majority of its observers.

Shying away from direct, personal contacts with the business, many accounts seem happy to base themselves exclusively on second-hand material: press cuttings, official statements, interviews with leading bureaucrats. In the place of concrete, historical realities – albeit observed with the inevitable distortions and inconsistencies of the participant view – we are presented with the monolithic 'objectivity' of official information sources. The 'truth' so established amounts, in essence, to a constant reformulation of certain stock themes – a renewed representation of previous representations, a never-ending progression of mirror images to the vanishing point where they clearly become *mis*representations.

This process had undoubted attractions for particular interest groups, who thus perpetuate a mythology of the illicit drug business which is as self-serving as it is inaccurate. Our quartet in the café in Cochabamba is a case in point: Guillermo's key role in the local scene depends above all on his privileged position of access to information generated within the trade. At the same time, his instinct leads him to exercise a certain discretion in matters relating to the economic wellbeing of his own operation, and that of the business as a whole. All information on prices, quality standards, supply routes and export initiatives is carefully screened, along with vital details such as the names of his protectors in high places. A few gems – news of an unique product, or of a particularly good price – are carefully released to his clients to indicate his expertise. His input into the mythology is that of the discriminating connection, the leader in market trends.

The other members of the group cultivate Guillermo for this kind of information, since it is a commodity more valuable than any amount of pink flake. Assuming, for the moment, that the American is in fact an undercover Drugs Enforcement Agency (DEA) operative, his interest will be in the sort of 'intelligence' which can be used to carry out seizures and arrests, to stem corruption and to pressure local governments. By its very nature, this intelligence will also undergo a screening process before being released to the public. Certain elements will be maintained as operational secrets, while others will be fed strategically into the world's information networks in order to achieve particular ends. This process of news management – determined by the political interests of the Western powers – thus further distorts the already partial view of the business provided by Guillermo and the other direct participants.

The journalist, on the other hand, is obliged by the nature of his profession to look for aspects of the business which will grab the attention of his readers. Sensational statistics, inflated financial estimates, scoop interviews and salacious scandals, blood-curdling busts and shoot-outs, are the standard fare of the media when dealing with cocaine. Serious investigative journalists (such as Gené)[2] may attempt to derive their information at first hand from dealers and local narcotics agents, but the vast bulk of what is published in newspapers worldwide has its origin in the big American press syndicates, when not directly in the DEA or the United States Information Agency (USIA). Needless to say, this only serves to perpetuate an extremely distorted and untrustworthy version of events.

We are left, then, with the historians and social scientists, whose general lack of imagination on the subject is underpinned by the fact that they usually situate themselves at the very end of this chain of misinformation. Working from dubious press sources and partial or biased official documents, it is not surprising that so little memorable material has yet been produced within the walls of academe. Field research of the participant/observer kind is virtually precluded by the difficulty in obtaining institutional support for what is perceived as an area of illegality. Equally, the conventions of scientific discourse stifle the emergence of a combative style of scholarship equal to the task of punching holes in the bombast of the anti-drugs campaigns.

Independent observers, however, should be able to confront the situation of near monopoly enjoyed by the official spokesmen on the illicit drugs trade. There is a clear need for some original and challenging polemic, one which reflects with greater honesty the perception of the real participants in the scene – the users, dealers and peasant producers – and which bases itself on a methodology of unsponsored and uncompromised research. Only in this way can it become sufficiently detached from the vested interests of the moment and actually chronicle the current changes. The moment is now; for in the case of South America, it is becoming evident that what we are witnessing is a major transformation of the economy, the onset of a new phase which will be known in future textbooks as the 'cocaine cycle'. It can be hoped that as cocaine 'comes in from the cold', knowledge and information on the subject is no longer limited to press releases of the DEA which clearly reflect a vested interest.

2. Cocainism: The Highest Form of Imperialism?

Creating a drug problem

While not denying that certain individuals do manage to get strung out on relatively unhealthy coke habits, it is clear that the purely medical aspects of the question have been given a quite disproportionate public emphasis. Disproportionate in comparison to the numerous intoxications produced by legal drugs and industrial pollutants, but disproportionate, also, to the immense human suffering produced as the result of the 'war on drugs'. Certain authors (notably Szasz)[3] have analyzed the ritual persecution of drug users and dealers in terms of a systematic scapegoating of certain deviant groups by an all-powerful medical establishment. Lest anyone think that this phase of pseudo-sanitary 'concern' has passed into history, consider the words of Edwin Corr, US Ambassador to Bolivia, in August 1984: 'One should look at the problem [of cocaine] as an illness, in the same category as malaria and other diseases.'

At the same time, the history of anti-drugs legislation provides an object lesson in how medical opinion (some of it, at least, well-intentioned) has not only served the narrow interests of the profession itself, but also has been manipulated for broader political purposes. Foremost among these was its symbolic role in resolving a conflict in the early part of this century between the declining European powers and a triumphant United States.

The Shanghai Commission of 1909, in which the Americans led a campaign against the British opium trade in China, provided a precedent for the world's earliest attempt at systematic drug control, the Hague Convention of 1912. Again at the instigation of the United States, this agreement instituted wide-ranging controls over cocaine – to the chagrin of Germany, whose pharmaceutical companies detained a virtual monopoly over the product at that time. It is no accident, therefore, that the expansion of US hegemony in this century has been accompanied by a parallel and simultaneous growth of the drug-problem industry.

Another important, but often neglected, aspect of problem creation is the erosion of traditional cultural controls over intoxication. In the unequal contest between 'backwardness' and 'civilization', the diffusion of an increasingly intolerant scientism or technological rationality provided a broader rationale for drug repression, thus diverting attention from the less palatable facets of US imperialism. Recent examples of this process range from the (as yet) unsuccessful attempts to criminalize the Amazonian hallucinogen *ayahuasca* or *yajé*, to the banning from Brazilian carnivals of a traditional aerosol spray known as *lança perfume* – an inebriating mixture of ether and ethyl chloride (chloroform).

It is, however, the case of coca leaves (still chewed by millions on the South American continent) which provides the most glaring example of this kind of pseudo-scientific moralism. In 1984, the US Congress Select Committee on Narcotics Abuse and Control could continue to make the stern recommendation that 'Peru and Bolivia should take steps to phase out the practice of coca-leaf chewing', apparently oblivious to the considerable body of research – much of it funded by US government institutions (viz. Carter *et al.*)[4] – into the cultural, nutritional and biological value of this custom. Though initially prompted by racist prejudice towards the indigenous population, the anti-coca lobby has also begun to target what was once considered a quite innocent facet of the question – the use of the leaves as a cure for altitude sickness and as an aid to digestion, practices which have long been acceptable even among the highly Europeanized middle classes.

In Peru, where the banning of coca would have been unthinkable as recently as ten years ago, the notorious government decree 22095 of 1978 has characterized the chewing of leaves as a 'grave social problem', thus paving the way to the criminalization of a substantial portion of the population. It should be pointed out that this change of legal status – with its ludicrous, quite unworkable prohibition of the use of coca below 1,500 metres altitude – was foisted on the population by a military government in the teeth of considerable local opposition. Its effects were soon being likened by leaders of the highland Indian communities to a *pachakuteq* (cataclysm) on a scale comparable to the Spanish Conquest of the sixteenth century, with the once-sacred leaf being converted into a symbol of criminality.[5]

The consequent disruption of traditional economic practices has been far-reaching, for with a ban on the possibility of returning from the coca-producing districts with a share of the harvest, highland workers no longer relish a descent into the unhealthy subtropical zone. The breaking of this basic barter link has also undermined the role of coca as an element of exchange in ritual practices and collective labour undertakings throughout Peru. It is difficult not to see in this a policy of deliberate ethnocide, with the DEA and the Peruvian government joining to destroy the politically inconvenient 'anomaly' of a healthy and culturally accepted form of drug consumption.

The response, too, has been equally virulent: strikes and demonstrations in the producing centres of Quilla-bamba and Tingo Maria led to the first national congress of coca growers in Cusco in 1980, held with the blessing of the local archbishop. Public protests have occurred at regular intervals ever since, and by 1984 Cusco's agricul-tural college had emerged as a focus of scientific opposition to American 'crop-substitution' projects, pointing out that many of the suggested substitutes, such as coffee and tobacco, were potentially much more damaging to physical wellbeing than the coca leaf.

This has not, however, prevented a radicalization in the position of the DEA-backed anti-coca lobby. By the early 1980s, a specialized police medical journal, *Revista de Sanidad de las Fuerzas Policiales*, could claim the existence of at least 3 million 'drug abusers' in Peru. On examining the statistics in detail, fully 98 per cent of the 'problem' population were found to be constituted by traditional users of the coca leaf.

Scapegoating on this scale quite transcends the usual practice of victimizing an unpopular minority. Forget the patter about 'deviant sub-cultures' – what we are witnessing here is an attempt to characterize an entire civilization as inherently and irredeemably fucked-up. Since the object of this kind of propaganda exercise is actually to avoid any real debate, the best 'problem' is often a vague problem – something distant, incomprehensible and alien, the threat of the unknown. Thus Brazilians are alerted to the growing 'menace' of khat (*Catha edulis*) abuse in the Red Sea states; presumably, Somalis are concurrently being educated to the threat posed by massive coca leaf 'addiction' in the Amazon.

Not only are traditional usages misrepresented, however; 'problems' are also created where they never existed previously. US consulates abroad arrange for groups of concerned parents to develop their sense of outrage at the plight of junkies in New York, glossy magazines print deliberately shocking pictures of the 'victims' with needles in their arms, and psychologists preach redemption and urge users to 'come forward with their drug problems'. In short, unsavoury drug habits are advertised and propagated worldwide, often by the same 'educational' programmes supposedly designed to prevent their emergence. Listing drug use as yet another element in the long list of threats to 'national security', institutionalized paranoia only serves to call forth demons and to feed them until they constitute veritable monsters.

It seems self-evident that the hypocrisy of the narcotics establishment – outrage at crops like cannabis and coca, silence on the subject of industrialized psychotropics – is prompted, above all, by the conflict of two rival systems within the framework of modern capitalism. If the pharmaceutical industry represents the establishment ('old money' and legitimate financial institutions), the illegal drugs business can be seen as a more daring and innovative sector – 'new money', associated with the advancement of previously submissive social groups. This simple dynamic, no different from numerous other phases in the regeneration of capital, cannot and must not be admitted to underlie the present dilemma. Hence the need to inculcate and stress repeatedly a concept of the drug 'problem' in accord with the perceptions of the developed countries. For instance, 1984 saw the American National Institute on Drug Abuse (NIDA) respond to the ever-burgeoning statistics on cocaine use with an upgrading of this substance to that of a 'powerfully addictive' drug. By this token, one must suppose that 'addiction' is defined as a side-effect of the unholy scramble for dollar bills.

In the late 1970s, it became apparent that the use of semi-refined cocaine sulphate (*base, sulfa* or *bazuco*) was beginning to spread among youthful, urban sections of the population in the producing countries. Smoked with tobacco or cannabis, the fumes of the sulphuric acid residue which this product contains have an undoubtedly deleterious effect on the lungs. At last the narcotics establishment could rest content; history had provided them with a real medical problem, an honest-to-goodness pathology that rendered the interminable debate about coca leaves so much old hat. The satisfaction was audible all the way to Washington: 'Other countries, unfortunately, have been forced to acknowledge that narcotics have become *their* problem, as well.' (George Shultz, US Secretary of State, September 1984)

Functional aspects of the war on drugs

That the drug 'problem' should appear insoluble is not, as the mass media would have us believe, the result of vicious scheming on the part of traffickers, nor is it a function of deep-seated 'weaknesses' in the psychology of the user population. Quite the contrary, this population – through the establishment of informal controls of the drug experience, the 'maturing out' of problematic consumption patterns, and the growth of numerous street agencies manned by people with first-hand drug experience – shows an inherent and spontaneous ability to generate its own adaptive response to novel forms of drug use.

Indeed, it is the anti-drugs establishment itself which requires that the problem should remain insoluble – not only to protect its own narrow interests in terms of funding and bureaucratic empire building, but also to push therapeutic services and rival pharmaceutical substitutes: methadone for heroin, imipramine for cocaine. In a particularly alarming new development, narcotics agencies are beginning to use the assets seized during operations as a means of financing their own day-to-day operations. By this means, a vested interest is created in seeing the situation snowball out of all proportion.

Furthermore, the universal perception of a huge (and always growing) drug 'problem', serves to legitimize a number of more straightforward political abuses. These range from the use of torture (as well-documented in drugs investigations in numerous Latin American 'democracies' as it was in the more traditional dictatorships), to the surveillance and victimization of certain troublesome individuals and social groups – not to mention the systematic infiltration of both the underworld and the local police forces by the Western intelligence agencies.

The drugs issue can also be used to destabilize Third World governments whose association with Washington risks becoming embarrassing. Such was the case of the unacceptably corrupt Garcia Meza régime in Bolivia in 1980, and, more recently, the Stroessner autocracy in Paraguay. Propaganda can likewise be directed at leftwing administrations – as has occurred at different times to Jamaica, Belize, Surinam, Nicaragua and the perennially unpopular Cuba. In a sense, such campaigns appear to be less a reflection of the extremely flimsy evidence than *prescriptive* statements, intended to act as self-fulfilling prophecies. In 1984, George Shultz claimed there was 'mounting evidence of the complicity of some Communist governments in the drug trade. Cuba uses drug smugglers to funnel arms to Communist insurgents and terrorists'.

In most other cases, however, the targets of such accusations are rogue sectors generated by the very contradictions of late capitalism itself. In early 1985 these have ranged from disgruntled, coup-prone ex-CIA officers in the Honduran general staff, to leading ministers in the Bahamas and the Turks and Caicos Islands, whose jealous defence of their countries' banking secrecy laws offended the DEA and the US financial establishment. The exposure given to such cases is very carefully managed, serving as a peg to promote veritable barrages of DEA-doctored information in the major communications media.

Every so often, however, something goes wrong in the otherwise well-organized management of the news. A good example was provided in 1981 by the involvement of one of Brazil's police chiefs in a massive pay-off from Colombian traffickers, a mere week after the American press had run long stories extolling the heroic efforts of his office in stamping out the cocaine trade. Equally entertaining have been the attempts to minimize a case rumbled in Spain in late 1984 involving the use of the Colombian diplomatic pouch to supply cocaine to a high ranking embassy official. The source of his supply was ultimately traced to a government functionary in the press office of the Colombian president, Belisario Betancur. This potential exposure of Betancur's image as a leader of the 'war on drugs' was buried by the media in a small half-inch note on the internal pages of the Latin American press. It is interesting to compare this treatment with the front-page spreads given to the largely undocumented accusations against Fidel Castro.

Accusations of corrupt practice can be deployed to force compliance with policies which are not even tangentially related to the drugs question. This function has become most evident in the attempted tying of military and development aid to a country's record in reducing drug production. First established during the Nixon presidency by means of the Rangel Amendment of 1972 – and subsequently strengthened by a new International Narcotics Control Amendment of 1983 – the threat to suspend aid for this reason has never yet been put into effect. This has not, however, prevented the State Department from using its annual narcotics report card to exert pressure on client states, often at the behest of particular interests with a strong lobby in Congress. The attempt to reduce Brazil's sugar quota in early 1985 provides a case in point: rationalized in terms of penalizing the country's growing participation in the illicit drugs business, it actually formed part of a trade war directed at a wide range of Brazil's exports – notably rolled steel and manufactured goods such as light aircraft, which were making serious inroads on the US domestic market.

The political interests served by the US media of drug-induced corruption are nowhere better illustratd than in the Mexican case. A a result of its paraquat spraying campaigns against cannabis and opium production, the country has received the approval of the US Congress and a generally good press. Little mention was even made of cocaine trafficking in Mexico until the end of 1984, depite the fact that Guadalajara is the base of operations of several large smuggling syndicates with an interest in the cocaine trade.

In February 1985, the DEA operative, Enrique Camarena, was kidnapped in Guadalajara and subsequently discovered dead. It was rumoured that Camarena was preparing a dossier that fingered leading *corruptos* in the police, the armed forces and the government bureaucracies. Alarmed that the war on drugs was beginning to rebound on its own agents, Washington reacted by sending heavily worded cables to the Mexican president and attorney-general, 'expressing frustration and disappointment' at the lethargy with which their investigations of the case were proceeding. Economic pressure was brought to bear as well. The State Department issued an official 'travel advisory' scaring away potential American holiday-makers, and the US Customs proceeded to work to rule on the international border, causing enormous traffic jams that destroyed overnight the booming Mexican export trade in perishable foodstuffs. The Mexican ambassador protested in Washington, the US ambassador in Mexico City protested back. By the end of February, the American media were citing DEA sources to the effect that Mexican gangs were responsible for 'approximately one-third' of all cocaine entering the United States.

Peru

Since it signed the notorious anti-coca decree of 1978, Peru has been favoured with a generally kind treatment from the DEA, the State Department and the Western press. As a means of signalling their approval of what are generally perceived as 'encouraging developments', official American estimates of the Peruvian coca crop remain static at around 60,000 metric tons, though independent sources calculate the real figure at two or three times this amount. Since 1980, the United States has been financing a special patrol unit called UMOPAR, dedicated to the repression of cocaine manufacture in the Huallaga valley. They are backed up by a US AID-funded crop substitution project (CORAH), whose budget in 1984 ($4.2 million) was used above all for military operations of forcible eradication.

This was not the original idea at all. CORAH had spawned an agricultural assistance arm (PEAH) which funded showpiece farms growing other crops in the middle of the main coca-producing districts. Peruvian peasants were supposed to learn from their example. The principal weakness in this strategy was that the PEAH farms depended on costly injections of foreign funding which were not available to the local population. The only access which local growers had to US AID funds was through the 'soft' loans offered by the Agrarian Bank, charged at a basic interest rate of 47 per cent plus a readjustment to account for inflation and the depreciation of the Peruvian currency (120 per cent in 1983). It is not surprising that so few coca farmers chose to switch crops voluntarily, for at a 167 per cent rate of interest nobody could afford to invest in any alternatives to the safer and more profitable coca bush.[6]

Resentment of this unappetizing carrot and stick policy

in the Huallaga valley surfaced in 1984 with repeated attacks on PEAH and CORAH installations. Significantly, their technological treasures (machinery, motorcycles, etc.) were dynamited, not stolen, making evident the total repudiation of this crop substitution project by the local population. The issue soon became more explicitly politicized with the involvement of Maoist guerrillas of the *Sendero Luminoso* group in co-ordinating the resistance. Slogans supporting *Sendero* had been evident on the walls of the area since early 1983, but in November 1984 they entered a phase of open insurrection with a force of approximately 100 guerrillas striking at three PEAH/CORAH bases and killing 23 employees. Fearful of a consequent escalation, the anti-coca campaign was suspended while the Peruvian Army began sweeping the countryside in search of *Sendero* activists.

Though the alliance between coca growers and Maoist guerrillas certainly suited US Secretary of State George Shultz's arguments about the emergence of a joint Communist/cocaine conspiracy, the situation would appear to be a little more ambiguous on the ground. In an interview with Gené in 1985, the local UMOPAR chief doubted that *Sendero* was effectively engaged in the illicit drugs trade, pointing both to the lack of any concrete evidence and to the fact that its weaponry was considerably less sophisticated than that of the cocaine cowboys.[7] Following a detailed study of *Sendero*'s history, Favre likewise considered that the extent of the guerillas' involvement was limited to imposing a 'revolutionary tax' on cocaine syndicates operating within its zone of influence.[8] In this context, the killing of unpopular CORAH agents by the guerrillas must be seen less in terms of a takeover of the trafficking network, and more as an attempt to capitalize on the social unrest created by coca eradication.

The Peruvian authorities, on the other hand, also had reason to be well pleased with the CORAH debacle. The outrage generated by the killings could be used to justify the continuing massacres of certain more combative sections of the peasantry. Furthermore, the notoriously corrupt regular army now had a justification to clip the wings of the US-supervised anti-drugs forces and resume its vocation of collecting unofficial tribute from the cocaine business. Finally, the heady coke'n'Communism mix would also serve the Lima government as a powerful tactical arm in its negotiations with Washington over Peru's debt and its need for fresh development funding. In short, upping the stakes in the coca wars suited virtually everybody – except, of course, the actual growers themselves.

Colombia

Similar contradictions also underlie the widely trumpeted 'fight to the death' undertaken by President Betancur in Colombia against the illicit drug trade. The assassination of his Justice Minister, Rodrigo Lara Bonilla, in May 1984, breathed new life into a programme of official collaboration with the United States which had begun in earnest in the late 1970s when the militarization of the Guajira peninsula – at that time source of at least two-thirds of the marijuana available on the US market – earned an accolade of praise from the DEA. It was obvious to any serious observer of that period, however, that the future for Colombian drug exports lay mainly in cocaine rather than in cannabis. By 1979, laboratories were being busted on the outskirts of Bogotá with stocks of 800 kilogrammes of refined cocaine, an enormous quantity by the standards of the time. Though domestic coca production has also increasedsubstantially in the last decade, the bulk of Colombian exports have traditionally been processed from crude base cocaine brought in from Peru and Bolivia. In early 1984, one such trans-shipment facility in the eastern department of Caquetá yielded a hoard of no less than $12\frac{1}{2}$ tons of cocaine.

The sheer scale of such operations quite transcends the type of garage-based cocaine economy which I described from the early 1970s in *Mama Coca*,[9] and which Brian Moser filmed in the Vaupés in the early 1980s for his *Frontier* trilogy (Central TV, 1983). Colombia is witnessing the emergence of extremely large and powerful trafficking syndicates: groups with the organizational skill to conceal over a ton of cocaine inside an air-cargo load of flowers into Miami, with the influence to maintain a permanent tap on the telephone communications between the Colombian Ministry of Justice and the US embassy, and with the political clout to set up meetings with their country's attorney-general in neighbouring Panama, in which they offered to give up smuggling, repatriate their assets, and help finance the national debt, in return for a complete amnesty.

Recruiting from the underworld, the police and the armed forces – or from the ranks of battle-hardened guerrillas disillusioned by their leaders' acceptance of the truce offered by President Betancur in 1983 – such groups are also consolidating their hold over the nation's financial institutions, adopting the role of populist social bene-factors through the funding of working-class housing and leisure facilities, and championing an anti-imperialist line in the time-honoured traditions of a national bourgeoisie.

In short, they are fast becoming the real power in Colombia.

President Betancur's major concession to Washington – the approval of extradition orders against several leading organizers of the trade – has seriously backfired, provoking a bomb attack on the US embassy and death threats which have led the American ambassador to resign his post, leaving the country in December 1984 along with over 2,000 other US citizens. Even the much-vaunted military hardware deployed on the Caribbean coast – mobile radars, nifty corvettes, high-altitude reconnaissance aircraft, helicopter gunships – can only, at best, interrupt exports for a short period, as Operation Hat Trick of 1984 showed. Before any seizures had been made, the smuggling groups succeeded in planting a story in the local press which gave away the operation's plan of action. The DEA was forced to concede that, as a result, their efforts were only 'modestly successful'.

Indeed, it would seem that many of the operations carried out in Colombia are determined as much by domestic US political concerns as by any realistic appraisal of their impact in South America. Spraying of Colombian marijuana fields with glyphosate herbicides, for example, was principally designed to allow the State Department an excuse to supply Congress with a warmly congratulatory account of Colombia's record in 1984, despite burgeoning cocaine exports. Equivalent tub-thumping has also been forthcoming from leading coke dealers themselves, many of them anxious in these days to protect their lives with a mantle of political legitimacy. In a recent interview with a Spanish film crew, Carlos Lehder – the organizer of paramilitary hit squads and founder of the fascist *Movimiento Cívico Latino Nacional* – went on

Colombian TV with the following statement: 'Cocaine and marijuana have become an arm in the struggle against American imperialism. We have the same responsibility in this – he who takes up a rifle, he who plants coca, he who goes out in public to denounce imperialism . . .'

In the face of the growing absurdity of the current scene and of its dangerous slide towards political instability, there is evidence of a certain retrenchment on the part of some Latin American governments. Perhaps perceiving that they are being sold a problem that will remain insoluble for ever – a veritable treadmill where every victory only heralds a yet more stunning defeat – the economically more resilient countries (notably Mexico and Brazil) are beginning to question the American obsession with 'interdicting' the supply of illicit drugs and are demanding an equivalent investment in the reduction of demand. Theirs is a variant of that old political cartoon: (South American president to Uncle Sam) 'It's not that we're corrupt, it's that you corrupt us.' It is a recognition of the realities underlying this change of heart, which no doubt underlies the oft-repeated defence of supply reduction as a foreign policy objective in the report of the Congress Select Committee for 1984.[10]

In defence of the strategy of crop eradication, the US points to its own campaigns against home-grown marijuana in which herbicides have been sprayed from the air – largely, one might add, on totally worthless stands of wild hemp in the state of Indiana. It also cites the creation of 13 regional anti-drugs task forces, while neglecting to point out that the oldest of these, in southern Florida, has failed to dismantle the local smuggling networks.

Moreover, a proliferation of final-stage cocaine laboratories has ecently been noted in the continental US. This development – in effect, a shift in the benefits of industrialization from the semi-periphery to the core area of contemporary capitalism – was precipitated by the very low cocaine base prices of 1983, and in 1984 by the DEA-instigated Operation Chemcon, a campaign designed to cut off supplies of ether and acetone to the laboratories in Colombia. In recent months, this campaign has spread to the other Andean states, to Paraguay and most recently to Brazil – the only country in South America with an installed industrial capacity to produce ether. In such circumstances, it is understandable that anti-drugs campaigns are beginning to be perceived in Latin America as a Trojan horse, acting to deflate local competition while at the same time encouraging competition in the States.

The Narcocracy: A Model for the Regeneration of Capital

Decomposition or recomposition?

How to characterize the 'narcocracy'? The first use of this term dates from 1980, the period of the Garcia Meza coup in Bolivia. It was used then to designate the idea of a political regime which drew its principal support from the illicit narcotics trade. Other authors, myself included, have subsequently used the word in a somewhat different sense, as a (largely deprecatory) form of shorthand to designate the various narcotics-related bureaucracies, and their staff of individual 'narcocrats'.

Droll they may be, but such usages do not do justice to the much wider implications of the growth of the illicit drugs business. For this reason, I would propose a more ample definition of narcocracy, one designed to include the numerous different sectors involved in the illegal trade – producers and consumers, processors and dealers, officials both corrupt and 'honest' – as well as all the subsidiary services which they generate, in a knock-on effect. In addition, I think it would be useful to distinguish between a formal narcocracy, such as the Garcia Meza regime – which, initially at least, made no bones about its intention to base its economic survival on the export of cocaine – and an informal or diffuse narcocracy, which is in fact historically the more common and characteristic type. The informal narcocracy would thus come to mean a political system which, no matter what its position in the left/right spectrum, is governed by a legal and ideological need to appear to be suppressing its principal economic activity, the production of illicit drugs.

Though he does not use the term himself, the work of Alvaro Camacho[11] provides a fruitful point of departure in characterizing what we will be calling the narcocracy. In describing the establishment of the coke- and dope-based dealing syndicates in Colombia in the mid-1970s, he began by calling into question the 'banana republic' model of the illicit trade which he felt underlay the relevant chapter in my earlier study *Mama Coca*.[9]

Rather than a simple alliance between the military and the traditional agricultural exporting sector, Camacho argued that the Colombian experience was marked by a process of accelerated and unequal capital accumulation which engendered novel class contradictions. The first of these was between the old oligarchy and an upwardly mobile 'emergent class' whose wealth was based predominantly, though not exclusively, on the illicit drug business. Within the oligarchy itself, he identified a further contradiction between a dynamic sector which defended the legalization of the drugs trade as a means to absorb 'new money' into established financial institutions,[12] and a more reactionary group, which followed the orthodox line on the 'war on drugs' dictated from Washington.

As a result of these contradictions, Camacho argued that Colombian society was facing a profound structural crisis. Not a crisis of the state – since this was being strengthened bureaucratically, ideologically and militarily by the monies being made available to 'crack down on drugs' – but a crisis of hegemony (between the different groups vying for control of government) and a crisis of legitimacy (between the regime and the dominated classes, who saw opportunism and corruption flourishing as the result of the illegal trade). He concluded that the resulting decomposition of the old bourgeoisie was likely to lead to the application of militarist solutions to social unrest.

His prognosis has been confirmed, at least in part, by the events of the last five years; for though President Betancur has managed to engender truces with many of Colombia's leading guerilla groups, he has found himself in an ever more ruthless war with the large trafficking syndicates. His inability to conclude this war with even a partial victory, however, renders evident the extent to which such campaigns are a structural feature of the broadly defined narcocracy. Official crackdowns do force leading dealers to withdraw into hiding, and they may require the relocation of processing facilities and the reorganization of smuggling routes. But they do not affect the continuing and growing turnover of the trade – nor do they prevent the drug overlords from continuing to buy their way into a country's military, financial and juridico-political establishments.

It may also be that Camacho's exclusive focus on

advanced sections of Colombian society results in an explanation which is inappropriate both to more backward regions of his own country and to the other Andean states. Colombia, after all, has a well-developed legitimate export sector, a thriving internal market and a level of industrialization more akin to Brazil and Venezuela than to Peru and Bolivia. In such a context, the idea of an 'emergent class' may have greater applicability than in the other main coca-producing nations.

Speaking of Peru, for example, Favre[13] describes 'a new division, more fundamental than the traditional opposition between classes, which it is tending to supersede. This division would oppose the integrated sector of the population (those with recognized 'jobs') to a non-integrated sector . . .' According to the Peruvian government's own statistics, the latter would include over half the economically active population, who find themselves forced to subsist by the hand-to-mouth logic of the 'informal economy' in which the diffuse narcocracy perhaps plays the preponderant part. In order to understand how this transformation of social realities has come about, it is instructive to consider in detail the attributes of the narcocracy in its most extreme and well-developed case.

Bolivia: last bastion of Mama Coca

'I don't think anyone should be ashamed or overly sensitive about the fact that if you have an illicit crop, and it's doing harm to people, that you're going to stop them growing it.' (Edwin Corr, US Ambassador in La Paz)

In order to acquire a first-hand familiarity with the major centres of coca and cocaine production I travelled in Bolivia for two months at the beginning of 1983. Notable changes were observable since the time of my first visit in 1971. Where cocaine had once been a secretive and marginal preoccupation, it was now rapidly becoming the major issue of the day. And where coca leaves had once been considered a mere folkloric curiosity, they were now the focus of intense nationalist passion – as if the whole population had been driven by circumstances to take stock of its traditions.

After two decades of military rule, Bolivia in 1983 was also enjoying the honeymoon period of President Siles Zuazo's left-of-centre UDP, a government whose non-interventionist principles allowed many sectors of society an unusual freedom of expression. In April 1985, this period seems to be drawing to a close, with a fragmentation on the Left and an imminent return to power of the traditional conservative parties.

Certain features of Bolivian life will, however, remain a constant. A principal element will be the almost universal consensus in the country on the value of coca as a national resource. Unlike the Peruvian case, where the coastal and urban inhabitants are largely speaking indifferent or unsympathetic to the traditional use of coca, virtually the entire population of Bolivia either chews coca, grows coca, or drinks coca-leaf tea. The urban bourgeoisie, the only potentially anti-coca social group, nevertheless are aware of the importance this plant and its derivatives have for the national economy, even if particular individuals are not themselves involved in the illicit trade. Coca production, after all, has been booming in a period of generalized economic decline. Though local statistics are notoriously unreliable, it seems safe to say that the coca crop has risen from approximately 8,000 metric tons in 1972, to 35,000 in 1980, 120,000 in 1984, and an estimated 170,000 in 1985.

The peasant population, particularly in the department of Cochabamba where most of this growth in production has occurred, have understandably become tenacious in defence of their main cash crop. On numerous occasion they have shown themselves capable of barricading the national highways in protest at official anti-coca measures, closing down economic activity with as much effect as a general strike. The most highly organized section of the labour movement, the miners, have for their part led demonstrations against poor quality and rising prices on the domestic coca market, arguing that high costs to the local consumer are part of a general policy to eliminate traditional coca use. In an initial environmental assessment of coca eradication programmes, even US AID officers were forced to concede that current policies 'will reduce the availability of coca to the traditional Indian users. Political impact will be high.' Perhaps for this reason, miners and peasants are also supported by a considerable body of opinion in the intelligentsia, the government services and even in the medical profession.

The last few years have thus seen a proliferation of groups constituted with the specific aim of defending coca from external pressures. The cautious Peruvian arguments in defence of traditional coca use have been taken one step further in Bolivia, where economists and peasant leaders now argue that the country should also be allowed to industrialize its coca crop legitimately. Pointing out that Coca Cola exerts a world monopoly on decocainized coca extracts and, through a subsidiary, has sewn up the world's supplies of pharmaceutical cocaine, the Bolivians defend the establishment of local processing centres to supply soft-drinks extracts, concentrated coca pastilles and legal cocaine.

It should be underlined that international law forces the Andean countries to spend hard-gained foreign reserves on buying synthetic procaine from the pharmaceutical giants, while they themselves are prevented from supplying the need for surgical anaesthetics with cocaine from their own native resources. In this context, Bolivians may be excused for thinking that the international criminalization of cocaine is primarily a means of enforcing an extremely inequitable balance of trade.

Coca and peasant social organization

In speaking of the peasantry which grows coca in Bolivia, one is not talking about a single monolithic formation but actually about two separate and clearly distinguishable social groups: one concentrated in the Yungas district of the department of La Paz, and the other in the Chapare, in the department of Cochabamba. Let us take the case of the Yungas first, since this more closely approximates traditional models of 'precapitalist' peasant production. An intensive form of agriculture is practised in this region; small bushes, rarely more than one metre high, are grown in serried ranks on steep, man-made terraces cut into the valleys at altitudes between 1,000 and 2,000 metres. The Yungas have been producing coca since Inca times, the local population being a mix of successive waves of colonization – Quechua and Aymara Indians, black slaves and white traders of diverse ethnic origins. Until the agricultural reforms of the 1950s, coca production was organized in medium and large-sized estates owned by absentee landlords, remnants of the colonial aristocracy of La Paz, who in the eighteenth and nineteenth centuries had succeeded in swallowing up the communal lands of the native communities.[14]

In recent years, individual families have worked private plots rarely more than one hectare in area, selling their produce to the government-licensed intermediaries who handle bulk deliveries to the highland towns. The flow of coca out of the Yungas has usually been controlled and taxed by an inspection post in the pass through the main ridge of the Cordillera Real. Given the nature of the terrain – no landing strips or alternative overland routes – this has generally kept local production at the mercy of the traders and the government of the day. Though controls have been lax during the Siles government of 1982–5, unlicensed coca trading was in other periods a virtual impossibility, as was acquiring a supply of the chemicals necessary to engage in autonomous refining of cocaine base.

Accordingly, the peasants of the Yungas are, by Bolivian standards, a generally submissive group, only rousing themselves to protest when threatened with a forcible reduction of the areas planted to coca. Since the potential for expansion is in any case pretty limited, most governments have seen fit to let well alone, being content to derive a modest income from taxes and the sale of trading licences. No doubt some of the leaves from the Yungas, on arrival in La Paz, are diverted from legitimate channels into cocaine production. Equally, the local processing of base in such towns as Coripata is no longer completely unknown. But the quantity involved is small, and the demand for Yungas leaves – considered the best for chewing – is such that they still fetch a competitive price in the unprocessed state.

The case of the Chapare, however, is in a different league. Though Chapare leaves fetch less than half the price of good Yungas coca, this is more than compensated for by higher standards of productivity – 959 kilogrammes per hectare annually, on average, as opposed to between 303 and 464 kilogrammes elsewhere. Chapare bushes are taller and more robust; they are grown in truly tropical conditions at around 250 metres altitude, on flat ground at the base of the Andes which does not require artificial terracing. In contrast to the Yungas, the Chapare is an area of recent colonization. In the 1930s, it produced less than one half per cent of the nation's coca, being sparsely inhabited and lacking a road over the mountains to Cochabamba. Disruption of the Yungas after the agrarian reforms of the 1950s, combined with a new highway to the Chapare built by the US in the 1960s, allowed this latter region to take over 65 per cent of national production by 1972, rising to 90 or 95 per cent today. These figures, calculated on the basis of official statistics, fail to convey a sense of the absolute increase in volume which has occurred – from approximately 3,000 metric tons in the early 1970s to at least 110,000 tons in 1984.

The population involved in this enterprise – currently around 100,000, with about three times that number of seasonal migrants helping with the harvesting, processing, transporting and other peripheral services – has adopted settlement patterns and forms of organization quite at variance with the stable peasant communities of the Yungas. Most retain a primary sense of loyalty to the highland communities where they originated, in the intermontane valleys of Cochabamba, or the high plateaux of Oruro and northern Potosí. There are few true villages in the Chapare, since colonization was determined by the pattern of land tenure, based on ten-hectare lots, each with a 100-metre frontage onto a local road. Colonists on a given stretch of road are organized into *sindicatos* ('unions'), which perform the services of local government – theoretically, everything from health and education, to the organization of a local defence force.

In practice, most public works have been delayed through the absence of government funding, itself based on a reluctance of the American-supported PRODES development project to supply anything (such as electricity) which might facilitate the production of cocaine. Not surprisingly, therefore, the *sindicatos* of the Chapare have tended to concentrate their efforts on defending their source of income, using their own militia to discipline criminal elements and keep the army and police forces at bay. Political activities have been concentrated on opposing the PRODES campaign of crop substitution, and on denouncing abuses by the narco-military complex when it has attempted to monopolize coca supplies (as occurred during the Garcia Meza dictatorship of 1980–81).

A pyramid of local political structures provides an arena for wider decision making. For example, a dispute in the early 1980s between the longer-established, pro-coca but anti-cocaine groups of the upper Chapare, and the unashamedly coca-for-cocaine group of the eastern Chapare and Chimoré, was resolved by 1983, when the numerical preponderance of the latter group, together with the phenomenal growth of the illicit market, made any repudiation of the cocaine business appear hypocritical and old-fashioned. No doubt the growing tendency for peasants to carry out the preliminary refining of coca leaves into base cocaine, as a means of deriving at least some of the benefits of the industrialization of their produce, played an important role in bringing about this change of emphasis.

Such an evolution raises important questions about the

nature of the 'peasantry' so involved. Blanes and Flores[15] have shown how a family-based economic strategy dominates coca production, mainly on account of the difficulty in organizing large teams of wage-paid labour. Only 16 per cent of growers cultivate more than one hectare of this crop – the area that can easily be maintained and processed by a single household – and larger plantations (rarely over three hectares) are worked with the help of more distant kin, brought in as migrant labourers from the highlands.

Nevertheless, even with the current booming output, there has been little capital accumulation in the area, beyond rudimentary house improvements and the purchase of a jeep or truck. The trade in cocaine base often remains tied to the most classic patterns of Andean economic reciprocity, being bartered along with coca leaves for food products brought in from other altitude zones. Significantly, such a system coexists with the hoarding of American dollars, since this is the currency used by the wider cocaine market. In financial terms, such hoarding is hardly 'capitalist' – the dollars constitute a reserve of symbolic value, not a productive investment expected to generate a profit.

Some authors, such as Canelas and Canelas,[16] have claimed that the profitability of the cocaine enterprise is leading to the emergence of an absentee landowning class in the Chapare. There seems to be little evidence to support this view, since the few absentee landlords in the district are mainly dedicated to the production of legitimate cash crops. Not only is coca production more efficient at the family level, it is also more difficult to eradicate than large, easily targeted plantations. There are also wider political reasons for maintaining the present situation: 'repeasantification' in the Chapare remains an important escape valve for a population suffering from a chronic shortage of land in the highlands, or from unemployment in the rapidly declining industrial and mining centres.

The American-funded PRODES development programme eems to have neglected to consider this aspect. Its reports intentionally underestimate the population in the Chapare, and continue to advocate the local establishment of large, well-capitalized 200–500 hectare estates, in imitation of the type of enterprise common in certain areas of Brazil, or of the United States. Obviously, such farmers would be more amenable to control through credit agencies and threats of legal action.

There is also a sense in which the debate on social and economic realities in the Chapare has been thrown off course by excessive reliance on a rigid opposition between 'capitalist' and 'peasant' forms of organization. Following Goodman and Redclift,[17] a synthesis seems possible which explains the emergence of local-level entrepreneurs in areas of smallholder agriculture. As a result of their prominence in the communal political structure, their diversification into cocaine base processing, their control of transport facilities and insertion in the wider regional markets centred on Cochabamba, such individuals would provide the indispensable middlemen between coca producers and the final-stage laboratory operators. Their example would serve to illustrate the opportunities for upward mobility provided by the cocaine business, and the consequent internal differentiation within the peasantry itself.

The first stage of the current cocaine cycle was characterized by bourgeois capital accumulation, based on control of processing and exporting facilities, and on the payment of locally determined prices for coca leaves, the raw material. Pressure from the primary producers for a greater share of the profits of the business, manifested principally by growing peasant involvement in cocaine base refining, has brought a new division of the spoils – with the large trafficking groups finding compensation for the erosion of profits in the enormous increase in the sheer volume of turnover. It is important to recognize that this change has been primarily a political conquest, resulting from peasant opposition to the high-handed practices of the cocaine establishment whose historical limits were reached at the time of the García Meza dictatorship. In this sense, the 'hands-off' policy of the Siles Zuazo presidency (1982–5) is revealed as consistent with its populist political position – it did effectively encourage an incipient democratization of the cocaine trade.

It is sadly ironic that the economic logic underlying this process – the filtering through to the peasant producers of a larger share of the world market value of their product – has so raised the value of coca within Bolivia itself as to place it, at $13 per pound in late 1984, quite beyond the purchasing power of its traditional consumers, the miners and peasants of the highlands. It remains to be seen if the strong links between the communities in the Chapare and their highland villages of origin can overcome the imbalance between coca producers and coca consumers. In truth, price differentials have always existed – coca in the southern highlands of Potosí has usually been worth three times its value in La Paz and Cochabamba[18] – and this has traditionally encouraged a great deal of internal smuggling past the government revenue posts.

Whenever official controls are imposed on the Chapare, as during the 'militarization' of mid-1984, an army of long-distance porters known as *cepes* (a species of leaf-cutter ant) find it economically viable to carry loads of coca leaf or base cocaine across the mountains to Cochabamba or Santa Cruz on tortuous trails over 100 miles in length. Furthermore, the very fact that over a quarter of a million seasonal migrants enter and leave the Chapare every year – arriving with highland products and returning home with their share of the leaf pickings – shows the continued vitality of the type of inter-altitude reciprocal trading and labour sharing which has long been such a notable feature of Andean life. It would be mistaken, therefore, to imagine that the cocaine business will ever be able to supplant completely the native coca trade, not least because the illicit market is fickle, whereas demand for coca is much more stable and continues to increase along with the Bolivian population itself.

Cocaine and Co: a profile of the bosses

Before considering the structure of the Bolivian cocaine industry, it is worth restating the two elementary features of the contemporary situation that have given this new economic cycle its enormous vitality. The first is the progressive decline of the legitimate export sector, a process beginning in mid-1970s and reaching significant proportions by the early 1980s when Bolivia's earnings fell from $1,037 million (1980) to $789 million (1983). The second inescapable truth is that the local value of cocaine is determined principally by the effects of the recurrent cycles of repression, in which one would include both DEA-inspired attempts at eradication, and military inspired moves towards monopolization. Lax controls and the resultant overproduction cause prices to fall, renewed pressure causes them to rise again. Prices for base (cocaine sulphate) in Cochabamba reflect this very clearly: from a high of $5,000 per kilo in late 1980, they fell back to as little as $300 per kilo in March 1983, only to rise again to approximately $1,000 per kilo by the end of 1984.

In their comprehensive analysis of the Bolivian cocaine industry, Bascopé and IEPALA[19] have produced a detailed history of this question, which provides conclusive evidence of the key role of the 1971-8 military regime in establishing the large trafficking syndicates. Beginning in 1973 with the INTERPOL-documented involvement of Health Minister Carlos Valverde – who ensured supplies of chemical solvents from his ministry, and tipped off his associates by leaking DEA plans – the action soon moved to the Santa Cruz-based Cotton Producers Association (ADEPA), an organization which represented the regime's closest allies among the wealthy landowners of the eastern lowlands.

Cotton prices were slumping, so many of the large ranchers of Santa Cruz and the Beni diversified into cocaine refining. The localities involved were a good distance from the Chapare, and tight security, organized on the basis of private bands of paramilitary thugs, was such that little news of the growing industry spread out of the area. The DEA played a key role in keeping the lid on these developments. Not only were denunciations at the time focused almost exclusively on the peasants of the Chapare, but to this day the 1971–8 regime has retained a clean image in the eyes of the Western press. By the late 1970s, three principal geographical centres had come to be constituted in the cocaine-exporting sector: the first in the San Javier/Portachuelo district, the second to the north in the Beni proper, and the third further south, around the town of Vallegrande. The local syndicates experienced considerable difficulties in penetrating the main market in the United States, as was shown when a senior member of the Santa Cruz business community was busted in Miami in 1980 with a shipment of 400 kilos of cocaine. As a result, Bolivian interests have mainly been forced to do business through Colombian inter-mediaries who prefer to undertake the final-stage manu-facturing themselves.

To make a profit, the prices for base in the Beni or Santa Cruz obviously had to be a good bit higher than in the Chapare itself. This has led to an internal, geographical price differentiation, with foreigners being encouraged to do business on remote landing strips in the eastern lowlands, yet being denied access to the primary pro-ducing centres. Here again the role of official military and police organizations, as well as shadowy paramilitaries, has been essential to the profitability of the overall enterprise.

The impunity with which the leading traffickers operate in Bolivia raises the question of the limits of state authority in the context of a diffuse narcocracy. Not a single government – whether of the Left, Right or centre, established by force or elected by popular vote – has been without scandal and well-documented cases of corruption, most often in the very organs supposedly constituted to repress the illicit drugs trade. Indeed, corruption may well be a misnomer in such a situation, and one should think instead in terms of *compenetration*. In this view, positions of official authority are the object of political contest in order to define who has the right to levy unofficial taxes on the cocaine business. A posting to one of the narcotics police forces – where salaries hover characteristically around a miserable 50 dollars a month – would thus still constitute a plum opportunity for the economic advancement of middle-echelon bureaucrats. The same would be true, for the younger officers, of a military command in the Chapare, the Beni or Santa Cruz.

It is becoming clear that this situation – where certain organs of the state act as parasites on the private-sector cocaine industry – is a more stable form of organization than outright hegemony. The experience of the Garcia Meza period was crucial in this respect: it showed that a formal narcocracy was subject to too many political crosscurrents to remain viable for any length of time. International pressures, principally from the State Department, caused a rapid erosion of the government's credibility, both abroad and within the country itself. Attempts to monopolize peasant production in the Chapare, and private empire building by government ministers, set different cocaine syndicates at each others' throats, leading to outbreaks of gang warfare. Not least, the control of government in La Paz brought the narcocrats into conflict with other sections of Bolivian society – from miners to bankers – each with their own private interests to protect, and their own particular capacity for causing disruption. Even the most cunning old hand in Bolivian politics would have found such a situation ungovernable – for the inept Garcia Meza and his associates, it was nothing short of disastrous.

Subsequent events, therefore, have seen a reversion to the type of informal or diffuse narcocracy which flowered in Bolivia during the Banzer years, and has likewise been the norm in Peru and Colombia since the early 1970s. Its applicability to the larger industrial economies, such as

Brazil and Mexico, may be restricted to less developed geographical regions and more marginalized sections of the population. But parallels in states with a weaker economic base – Jamaica, Belize, Ecuador, Paraguay – are already clearly apparent, and will no doubt become more pronounced in the case of a further decline in the legitimate economic activity of these countries. The system of informal narcocracy allows the government of the day to continue paying lip service to the 'war on drugs' while favouring its own private interests and arming an anti-narcotics force which can be used in the task of selective victimization of its political enemies.

Though the narcocracy as an arrangement may only have a limited life span, its overthrow or transcendence will require either a substantial increase of agricultural credit and industrial investment – which seems unlikely in the current economic climate – or serious reforms in the drugs laws and a major realignment of political and strategic loyalties. Given the hysterical reaction of the United States to even the most tentative socialist experiments, let alone the legalization of cannabis and coca exports, these options appear hardly more likely than the revival of the free-spending Alliance for Progress. For these reasons, I would argue that the informal narcocracy is becoming a leading if not the the predominant form of social and political organization in many parts of late twentieth-century Latin America.

Double Standards and the Single Convention

A paradox underlies the 1961 Single Convention on Narcotic Drugs. How is it that an instrument designed to reduce the use of illicit drugs can ultimately have ushered in an age when the consumption of these substances has increased beyond even the most alarmist projections? Is it not obvious that the misconceived obsession with extirpating the use of certain drugs – those deemed illicit – greatly increases the profitability of their production?

The decline in Bolivia's legitimate international coca trade demonstrates the reverse side of this coin – the damage done to the traditional beneficent forms of drug consumption. A large market for Bolivian coca has existed in the northern Argentine provinces of Salta and Jujuy since the Inca conquest of that area in the late fifteenth century. This trade remained substantial throughout the colonial and early republican periods, and grew further at the turn of the twentieth century with the rapidly expanding demand generated by migrant highland labourers in the sugar plantations of Argentina and the nitrate fields of northern Chile. In the period 1900–1920, up to 30 per cent of total Bolivian coca production went to markets in these neighbouring countries.

Attempts by Chile (1927) and Argentina (1932) to ban the importation of coca leaves under the terms of the Geneva Convention of 1925 were unsuccessful, due both to a vigorous defence of the trade by the influential landowners of the Yungas, and to a desire by local Chilean and Argentine magnates to defuse the Indian labour force's resentment of their appalling working conditions. British and American firms active in northern Chile and Argentina went along with this view. Between the wars, coca tea was served in the cricket pavilion to British expatriates running the large sugar mills of San Pedro de Jujuy, and as late as the 1970s polite circles in Salta still chewed coca leaves as an after-dinner digestive. Coca was thus considered a beneficent plant by the population of northwestern Argentina – being enthusiastically adopted even by recent immigrants such as the Syrian shopowners – a fact commented on with some surprise by numerous contemporary visitors from Buenos Aires[20].

The spread of criminalization was slow but inexorable. Prohibition of coca had begun in Chile in the early 1950s as the result of pressure from the UN. Argentina, however, continued to allow coca legally into its two northern provinces until 1976, a year in which they took 800 metric tons of leaves. But by now different social forces were at work in the Andes: the sugar industry was in decline and patrician landowners no longer ruled the roost. Corrupt officialdom, allied to dynamic sectors of the growing black economy, could begin to use American pressures for criminalization to their own advantage. In strictly economic terms, the old-style coca trade could no longer compete with a cocaine-based illicit economy that had grown up in the 1970s.

It should have come as no surprise, therefore, when the new military regime of General Videla in 1977 banned any further legal coca imports. The incipient narcocracy of Salta and Jujuy was thus able to extend its control both to the illicit production and trans-shipment of cocaine through Argentina, and to the traditional coca trade whose new-found illegality brought higher prices and thus greater profitability. In Salta in 1983, coca was still easy available, being sold surreptitiously in the marketplace, under the watchful gaze of the local plainclothes police/mafia, and at prices ten times higher than in Bolivia. This clandestine trade accounts for the large quantities of coca which still show up in official Bolivian statistics as being supplied to the insignificant frontier townsof Uyuni (for Chile) and Villazón (for Argentina).

The sub-imperialist strategy

The Argentine case is significant not only because of the opportunity it has provided for developing alternative export routes for Bolivian cocaine. More importantly, it provides an example of how small regional economies – such as the coca trade in Salta and Jujuy – can be swamped by wider international trends. In addition, corrupt bureaucracies everywhere could learn from the system of divided responsibilities operating in the area, with numerous federal and regional police forces, rival military units and judicial bodies all blaming each other for the continued growth of contraband.

Indeed, with the growth of the cocaine trade through Argentina during the years of the military dictatorship, it should come as no surprise that the authorities in Buenos Aires soon became vociferous supporters of the continent-wide 'war on drugs', adding to the general paranoia a number of flourishes entirely of their own inspiration – such as the theory that the majority of 'terrorist' attacks were carried out under the influence of drugs. That continuing abuses of the drug-using public should now be taking place under a freely elected government which in many other respects has taken a courageous line of opposition to Washington, only shows how far the criminalization and depoliticization of the drug question has been allowed to go.

What are the implications of the emergence of official 'alarm' in a supposedly independent and more nationalistic centre such as Buenos Aires? One function may be to provide spokespeople for arguments that even the DEA would have difficulty in defending in public. Such was the case of Dr Cagliotti,[21] who at international conferences espoused the view that coca chewing leads to an evident degeneration in 'intelligence, attention and personality' and the development of a 'repellent aspect' in its adepts. In view of the considerable resentment being created by the US government's insistence on crop eradication in the producing nations, it was inevitable that surrogate leaders would have to be found within Latin America itself to give the campaign against coca the credibility it so obviously lacked.

International bureaucracies have also played their part: the UN hosts a plethora of narcotics-related bodies who follow the line dictated from Washington, while the Organization of the American States called in 1984 for the establishment of a co-ordinated regional anti-drugs campaign. The problem with all such multilateral organizations, however, is that they are clearly perceived to be little more than the DEA riding under assumed colours. For this reason, any recourse to international armtwisting must make use of strong local allies to put forward the DEA's views.

Mexico and Venezuela have each played this role in their own particular regions despite repeated scandals implicating their police and armed forces in sizeable illicit transactions. Argentina provides an important lever for use in the southern Andes, though this has little impact on the main flow of cocaine northwards to the United States. This leaves one major candidate, Brazil, as the principal defender of American interests in the southern hemisphere, a part which it was happy to play on numerous occasions and in widely varying contexts throughout the two decades of military rule between 1964 and 1985. On the drugs issue, it has promoted bilateral treaties with

Colombia and Peru (May 1984) and Venezuela (January 1985). Acting with overt DEA support and encouragement, such treaties are designed to facilitate mutual extradition, 'hot pursuit' across international boundaries and the sharing of intelligence.

In the specific case of the cocaine business, Brazil offers several strategic advantages to the DEA. Firstly, it shares common borders with the main producing countries and has a growing importance as an alternative refining and trans-shipment centre, particularly in the western Amazon region. Occasional busts of small laboratories, plus the growing demand for cocaine on the domestic market, can both be used to fuel alarm in the local media and government bodies. At the same time, the traditional use of coca – although still common in certain remote regions – is still sufficiently distant from the cultural experience of most Brazilians to preclude the formation of any vocal pro-coca lobby, such as those which exist in the Andean nations.

There are other advantages, as well. The enormous internal production and consumption of *maconha* or *diamba* (cannabis) can be spotlighted whenever there is need to pressure Brasilia into accepting DEA recommendations. Certainly, the DEA is unlikely to welcome the consequences of the political liberalization currently taking place in Brazil. Numerous public debates and the odd publication (viz. Henman and Pessoa, 1985)[22] have raised the question of decriminalizing the use of cannabis, pointing out that the severe repression of this plant during the military dictatorship both ignored its long history of use among the black population and failed to prevent its adoption since the 1960s in virtually every corner of the country, every walk of life.

Cocaine, too, has been consumed in elite and bohemian circles in Brazil since the turn of the century, and Rio and São Paulo remained outlets for the product even in the period, 1935–65 when it virtually disappeared in other major Western cities. The growth of consumption in the 1970s paralleled and reflected trends elsewhere in the Americas, and today Brazil probably represents the single largest national market outside of the United States.

This gives the DEA the most perfect excuse for using the Brazilian Federal Police to its own advantage: sometimes as an arm to root out corruption in the local police forces (many of which have long records of 'fiscalizing' the illicit trade), and on other occasions, as a means of bringing pressure to bear on the Bolivians, the Peruvians and, principally, the Colombians. To understand how such a development has been possible, it is necessary to look at recent events in the border area between Brazil and Colombia.

Breeding monsters: coca eradication in the Amazon basin
Coca has long been a basic element of the diet and customs of numerous indigenous groups in the northwest Amazon, providing not only vitamins and scarce mineral trace elements but also the principal focus for much social activity. Coca is chewed while hunting, fishing, canoeing, felling the forest and digging the earth. Among the Tukano and Makú of the Rio Negro, coca is chewed nightly by most adult men in order to facilitate conversation and to 'remember the ancients' through myth recitation. Two or three hours a day are dedicated by most men to the laborious process of making the local *ipadú*, a coca powder produced by pounding and sieving the leaves with an ash admixture. Coca is also a central

element of shamanic healing practices and collective celebrations, serving to prevent drowsiness during all-night rituals, and providing a balance to the alcohol, tobacco and hallucinogenic *caapi* drink consumed on these occasions.

It is important, however, not to have an excessively romanticized view of the use of coca in the northwest Amazon. There is, in fact, a larger population of coca chewers to be found outside of the traditional indigenous setting among the rural population in the vicinity of Tefé – a town located just off the main course of the Amazon some 400 miles from Leticia, Colombia's main river port and a well-known centre of the cocaine business. The local inhabitants are mainly composed of the descendants of refugees from the atrocities of the turn-of-the-century rubber boom in the Caquetá and Putumayo drainages. Though predominantly Indian in stock, this population has largely lost the distinctive languages and social practices which mark off tribal peoples from the broad mass of the population. In such a context, the use of coca has an important role in establishing the ethnic identity of the native-born in the face of more recent waves of immigration.

Coca in this region might have remained little more than a local curiosity, were it not for the sudden growth in cocaine processing across the border in Colombia. Though the alkaloid yield of Amazonian coca is lower than that of the main Andean species, it has the advantage of growing quicker and more profusely, as well as being propagated by cutting rather than by seed, which represents a considerable saving in labour. I travelled in the Rio Negro in 1979, and in the region of Tefé in 1981, just as both of these areas were awakening to the implications of the new economic circumstances: the opportunity they presented for the production of coca as a cash crop, and the darker side of the same coin, the intimidation which they invited from Colombian dealers and the Brazilian Federal Police.

Strangely, it was in the remote districts of the Rio Negro that the Brazilian authorities first began their campaign to eradicate coca. No doubt the highly intolerant Salesian missionaries of this area, who had been campaigning for years against the use of the drug, have much to be credited for in this curious turn of events. From 1980 to 1982 the local press carried regular stories about the discovery of 'vast plantations' in the area, none of them corroborated by any of the few independent witnesses who visited the Indian villages during that period. It is true that the early 1980s witnessed a short-lived boom in base cocaine production in the neighbouring Colombian region of the Vaupés, and possibly a few sacks of leaves did cross the border at this time. This phase ended, however, in late 1982 as the result of falling cocaine prices and the high cost of flying in chemical supplies by air. On a visit to Brasilia in November 1983, Indian leaders from the Rio Negro countered accusations about their involvement in the trade with an observation that prices were so low it would be unprofitable to plant coca for any other use than chewing.

At about this time, however, the emphasis of the Brazilian Federal Police shifted to the region around Tefé. Since the local population could not claim the privileges of cultural autonomy accorded to tribal Indians, there was never any question in Tefé of the authorities conceding that at least some coca should be allowed for domestic consumption. All coca in Tefé was decreed illegal, and an 'educational' exercise was undertaken to instil the idea that coca chewing was backward, depraved and unhealthy, and that anybody who grew coca had to be working hand in glove with the Colombian 'Mafia'. Major campaigns of crop destruction using DEA-supplied gunboats, helicopters and flame-throwers, were sent out in late 1983 and again in late 1984. If one is to believe official estimates, over 6 million bushes were destroyed in 1984 alone.

It must be stressed that both operations were under-written and directly overseen by US narcotics agents. Their presence was so overwhelming within the Brazilian Federal Police that the head of its drug division, Hugo Póvoa, resigned in November 1984, claiming that 'every-thing we have done, has been with American money'. Far from being resentful of his Yankee bossses, Póvoa seems to have taken their side, complaining at the lack of funding from his own government and demanding the institution of a drugs force independent of the Federal Police and directly modelled on the DEA. It seems likely, therefore, that the subordination of the Brazilian Federal Police to policies dictated by the US will continue with Póvoa or without him, and should easily survive the transition to a right-of-centre democratic government.

The early months of 1985 have already seen pressure building on Brazilian suppliers of ether and acetone, and search-and-destroy operations against clandestine labor-atories and coca plantations are moving in closer to Leticia. With *Sendero Luminoso* guerillas from Peru supposedly sighted on the frontier, the scene is being set for a major conflagration on the upper Amazon, involving everyone from highly sophisticated cocaine operators and the police and military organizations of four countries (USA, Brazil, Colombia and Peru), to totally uncontacted

Indians on the headwaters of the Javarí river. At the very least, it seems clear that techniques of coca eradication are being tested in Brazil on a scale that would be politically unacceptable in the Andean countries. From a springboard in a nation with little or no understanding of the plant, the DEA could be preparing 'options' for an offensive on the traditional strongholds of the coca leaf – a move which would convert the 'war on drugs' into true economic warfare and ultimately into a war between states.

After all, what are the 'options' open to the DEA? Mechanical eradication – uprooting and burning of the bushes – is efficient, though it is also labour-intensive, dangerous and pitifully slow. Spraying with herbicides remains a possibility, though the levels of dosage required – even of strong compounds such as 2,4,5 T or 2,4 D – are so high that widespread poisoning of the environment would result. Most technical assessments (viz. U.N. 1979)[23] therefore consider this approach unacceptable, though in 1982 2,4 D was given a highly controversial trial by the DEA in the Yapacaní region of Bolivia, and has also been tested more recently in Colombia and Peru. These difficulties have forced the Brazilian authorities to reassess their strategy. What they *are* preparing the ground for is a wholly new departure, first announced to the press in October 1983; the use of biological weapons against coca.

The Brazilian agricultural research agency EMBRAPA has already received a budget of $3 million to develop and adapt new, 'coca-specific' fungi, bacteria, viruses and insects, cultures of which they are no doubt receiving even now from the DEA. It is argued that such methods of crop eradication are 'pollution free', though one shudders to think what the bugs will eat when they run out of coca leaves. More significant than the terms of the official debate, in any case, are the items deliberately excluded from discussion.

What is never pointed out is that such agents (whether polluting or not) have a much wider geographical range of action than the herbicides. Indeed, what is to prevent a coca pathogen, once released in Brazil, from straying across the border into neighbouring countries? Perhaps the DEA's greatest threat lies here: the annihilation not only of the major commercial producers but of any remnant pockets of healthy coca use, so that even the most lowly peasant, the most isolated Amazonian Indian, can all become fully integrated hostages of the insoluble cocaine 'problem'.

Cocaine Futures

Before addressing the complexities of the blackmarket economy, let us return to consider the café in Cochabamba and the meetings taking place between representative figures in and around the cocaine business. At a quite different gathering from the one originally described Guillermo might be sitting with true professional contacts. What would be the nature of their discussion? *Prices.* Prices for leaves, at source and in town, prices for base in the Chapare or in Cochabamba, prices for refined cocaine in La Paz and Santa Cruz, in Lima or São Paulo, in Bogotá, New York and Amsterdam . . .

Unlike a legitimate commodity market, however, there is no daily wire service to provide punters with a constant update on cocaine price movements. Press accounts are virtually always inaccurate, grossly overestimating the value of a given shipment by the simple expedient of relating it to some fictional price on the street in New York in grams cut at 30 per cent purity. Even on the underworld grapevine, price assessments are by no means an accurate reflection of the true value of transactions – many of which take place at special discounts for friends and old customers and bona-fide non-narks.

It is hardly surprising, therefore, that participants in the market should be so concerned with cultivating contacts and finding out about prices, and thus mapping the profit margins between leaf and refined toot, or between the Chapare and the affluent urban markets. The survival of an individual entrepreneur depends upon his ability to insert himself at some particular point in this sequence, buying cheap and selling dear and minimizing overheads such as processing and transport costs, not to mention bribes. In this process, the street-side cafés of Cochabamba play a role similar to that of the coffee houses of seventeenth-century London – a source of gossip and rumour for those involved in the trade.

It is interesting to compare this set-up – which actually works as an information system, despite the complete absence of hard data – with the utter confusion reigning in the narcotics bureaucracies themselves, whose main concern is less with prices and more with estimates of total production. Despite its cult of intelligence, its satellite surveys and its blithely confident statistics, the DEA almost never gets it right. The case of the 10,000-ton marijuana bust in Chihuahua in 1984 provides a good example. That such an enormous plantation had reached maturity so close to the US border must have raised serious questions about the much-vaunted efficiency of satellite-based aerial photography in detecting illicit crops. Cannabis, after all, has a clearly defined colour signature and cannot be grown under the shade of larger plants.

In the case of coca the problem is much more acute. Recently picked coca bushes do not show up in aerial photographs at all, and even leafy bushes have a colour signature which can be confused with those of plantain, coffee and cassava which are grown in similar environments and often in the midst of the coca plantations themselves. A consistent underestimating of production in the late 1970s and early 1980s – dictated by political reasons such as encouraging governments friendly to the US – produced a situation in 1984–5 where estimates had to be revised dramatically upward, making it seem that production has increased two or threefold in each of the previous couple of years. In the case of Colombia, for example, the DEA had estimated for 1984 a total production of 35 metric tons of cocaine hydrochloride. Just in the first eight months of that year, Colombian authorities seized over 33.5 tons – without creating any appreciable shortage on the American market.

The inaccuracy of official estimates also serves to heighten the instability of the cocaine market. After a period of gradual, constant and sustained increases in prices and production during the 1970s, the period 1980–85 has witnessed sharp price fluctuations, produced as the result of alternating gluts and shortages, in the classic boom-and-bust cycle of many other tropical products. Prices for a kilo of cocaine base in Bolivia have varied between $300 and $5,000 – the latter figure being reached at the height of the 1980–81 boom, the former at the bottom of the slump of 1983. Characteristically, there is a time lag down the supply network and fluctuation is less extreme the closer one approaches the consuming centres.

Thus, a kilo of refined cocaine in Medellín, Colombia, rose to $20,000 in mid-1982, only to fall back to $4,000 by early 1984. In the United States, the equivalent figures were $60,000 and $16,000 – representing, to the consumer, the difference between a $100 and a $50 gram, as well as a rise in street-level purity from an average of 12 per cent to an average of 30 per cent.

This situation bears many points of comparison with the traditional commodity trades before international agreements and telecommunications links effectively removed the possibility of profitable arbitrage between different trading centres. Not surprisingly, therefore, some of the same instruments of commerce have emerged in the cocaine market to protect investors from sudden price fluctuations.

In Cochabamba, in early 1983, I discovered that insiders in the city's drugs trade were operating a system of futures – verbal contracts, accepted on trust, to deliver a specified quantity of cocaine at some future date. Cash was paid up front; in full generally, though sometimes in part, echoing the development of 'margin payments' and 'options' on the legitimate futures markets. The system was of benefit to investors who could thereby buy cocaine for forward delivery at prices which were, on the 'spot' market of the time, extraordinarily low. It was also useful to the sellers/manufacturers who could thus continue producing without cash-flow problems and the fear that the generally slack market of 1983 would cause them to close down. But who were the biggest beneficiaries of all?

In order to operate efficiently, a system of futures requires safe stockpiling of the product. In the case of the Bolivian cocaine industry – which, at the time, was also using hoarded stocks to depress the prices paid to peasant base producers – we are talking about a quantity of several tons. This represents an exposure running into tens of millions of dollars, and all the while without the benefits of insurance, should something go wrong. For this reason, it was imperative that those syndicates which emitted 'contracts' for future delivery of cocaine should be able to shield themselves from official intervention, DEA intrusion, peasant appropriation and thieving from rival organizations. They had to be big, and they had to be powerful.

Illicit commodities and the acceleration of capital

The growth of cocaine-based capital structures must be situated in their social and historical context. Latin America, and particularly the more fragile, less industrialized societies of the Central Andes, are currently passing through a severe crisis of recomposition, both in their economies and in their political life. Recent research in Peru, for instance, indicates that more than 60 per cent of the working population earn their living in an 'informal' sector which functions entirely outside the official economy. Though untaxed, ununionized, and unregulated, this economic 'underground' accounts for 95 per cent of Lima's public transportation, 90 per cent of the clothing industry, 60 per cent of the construction trade. Though its most visible face is the crowd of street vendors populating the major cities, it also involves a number of high-technology enterprises, ranging from motor-vehicle assembly to the manufacture of precision instruments for the air force.

It is important to understand the need for an accelerating rate of capital accumulation under such circumstances.[24]

The survival, that is, the growth, of national capital in 'Third World' countries demands a higher rate of return than that obtainable on the world's leading financial markets. It has also generally implied a retreat from productive or industrial activities and a return to the more traditional patterns of speculation employed by merchant capital, notably in the basic commodity trades.

The involvement of part of the local capitalist class in cocaine production provides a good example of how this process of economic retrenchment has occurred. Cocaine is an attractive form of merchandise; the fact that it is consumed easily and to relatively little effect means that it has no need of an obsolescence factor – it has a naturally rapid turnover. The high risks of the illicit trade also justify a sizeable profit margin based on selling dear to affluent customers (exploiting the surplus value of productive capital) and buying cheap from local growers and base manufacturers (exploiting the surplus product of non-capitalist producers).

Such has always been the logic of merchant capital; what is unique in the illicit drugs trade is that repressive laws have generated an exaggerated profitability in what would be otherwise a rather sluggish and superseded form of economic activity – primary commodity trading. The crisis in the mid-twentieth-century development model has thus generated a response which is both archaic (commodity production) and innovative (the predominance of an illegal trade within the general context of a growing 'informal' economy). For this reason, the current crisis, and the apparent threat it poses to legitimate financial institutions, should in fact be seen as offering a new basis for local capitalist expansion.

In considering the extreme case of Bolivia, we can see

what the consequences of this turn have been. In Bolivia, the local exchange market is composed of two sectors: one official, providing dollars at government-decreed rates in order to pay for essential imports, the other unofficial ('black' or 'parallel'), buying and selling dollars at the rate decreed by the market. Given that by far the larger part of the dollars circulating in Bolivia have their origin in the cocaine trade, it is perhaps not surprising that the only temporary decline in the unofficial exchange rate in recent years – the dollar has otherwise risen constantly, from 40 *pesos* in October 1982 to 55,000 *pesos* in October 1984 – was registered between February and June 1983 when local cocaine prices were going through a rare bad patch.

The unofficial exchange market, then, can be seen to act in effect as a single vast money-laundering operation. The cocaine-earned dollars are used to finance an equally flourishing contraband trade in the other direction, which supplies Bolivia with a range of products: basic necessities and industrial goods from neighbouring countries such as Brazil and Argentina, gadgetry and luxuries supplied from all over the world, and funnelled through the free-trade zones in Panama and Paraguay. There can be no doubt that the volume of this traffic greatly exceeds that of the official trade statistics, which showed a decline in legitimate export earnings from $1,037 million in 1980 to $788 million in 1983. By 1984, it was calculated that the Bolivian state had to find 60 per cent of the cost of its essential imports, due to the introduction of differentials in the official exchange rate – a higher rate for exporters, and a lower rate for importers – designed to encourage exports and thus reverse the decline in legitimate foreign earnings. In the absence of foreign loans, the resulting deficit could only be covered by buying dollars on the unofficial exchange market, a policy which in turn required the printing of more *pesos*. The result was the galloping inflation of late 1984, which by year's end was approaching an annual rate of 3,000 per cent (up from 500 per cent in 1982).

What this means is the slow disappearance of a national currency and any vestige of an autonomous national economy. Industrial production fell by 17 per cent in 1984, and mining output by a similar figure. The 756 per cent salary increase accorded to the miners in the nationalized sector in December 1984 was correctly perceived by most union leaders as little more than a joke – within a couple of months the miners were back on strike, holding massive demonstrations in La Paz. *Peso*-denominated prices for even the simplest products are now so volatile that it has become standard practice for traders to fix prices in dollar terms and employ a daily-changing multiplication rate for those who wish to pay in local currency. Often this is no longer necessary – in some of the cocaine-rich districts around Cochabamba, pounds of potatoes are now changing hands for dollar bills . . .

There is little any government can do to alter this situation. A payments moratorium on the foreign debt, adopted in mid-1984, means that the credit-worthiness of Bolivia's central bank, even to its own citizens, is virtually nil. In mid-1984, the launching of dollar-denominated savings certificates – in effect, an attempt by the government to offer a money-laundering service rivalling that of the unofficial exchange market – failed to attract much attention, despite higher interest rates than could be earned in New York at the time. Cocaine money was unwilling to launder its narcodollars through the acquisition of paper so lacking in credibility. The only takers were local banks with debts to foreign creditors, since by acquiring these certificates they effectively made the bankrupt state assume responsibility for Bolivia's private debt.

The financial contradictions generated by the cocaine business are not, however, necessarily identical in every country. In Colombia, whose legitimate economy remains relatively buoyant, the banks had long operated a no-questions-asked 'side window' (*ventanilla siniestra*) which accepted and exchanged foreign currencies of any origin. Though this never absorbed more than 10 to 20 per cent of the country's illicit drug earnings, the volume of deposits involved was sufficient by the early 1980s to threaten a takeover of several major banks and credit companies.

The nervousness of these institutions was compounded by the fact that a growing parallel finance market had come into existence in Colombia. As early as 1977, 10 per cent of all business loans were estimated to have their origin in this loan-shark sector. Given the growing misgivings in 'straight' financial circles, as well as the prodding of the United States, President Betancur decided in 1983 to institute much stricter exchange controls. As a result, more drugs funds than ever before remained outside the country leading to undercapitalization where there was once overcapitalization and thus to inflation and renewed penetration by foreign capital in the nation's industrial and banking sectors.

Peru represents something of an intermediary case. In the late 1970s, some of the profits of booming cocaine exports were absorbed through the issuing of dollar-denominated government bonds – which remained relatively attractive as long as the Peruvian state continued creditworthy. For a time, dollars were so widely available and easily converted that the blackmarket exchange rate in such cocaine-rich towns as Tingo Maria was actually *below* that paid by the banks and the government – presumably to cover the costs of moving dollar bills across the Andes to Lima and the hassle of laundering them through the banking system. This situation could not survive the heavy doses of IMF medicine in the early 1980s, however, and the Peruvian central bank now seems set to follow its Bolivian counterpart down the slope to insolvency. Senior Western bankers appear to view this development with relative equanimity – from their perspective, it is more important to prevent a default by Brazil, Mexico or Argentina and simply let Peru and Bolivia 'fall by the wayside'.

Such a development can only encourage a further bout of generalized asset stripping in the official economies of the Central Andes, coupled with the triumph of the informal sector – its growth to the point where it becomes, in fact, the 'true' economy of the area. In a microcosm, exactly this process has already occurred in the coca-producing districts of the Huallaga basin, in central Peru. US AID money, supplied for the voluntary eradication of coca, has almost all been used to buy up and destroy not the viable, illicit plantations of coca, but the legal patches grown with government licence – most of them 'aged bushes no longer providing worthwhile yields'.[25] Officially grown coca must be sold to the state monopoly ENACO at prices decreed by the central government, which are often less than half those paid by cocaine refiners. Like most of the legitimate economy, the production of coca under these terms is virtually a loss-making venture. Even from the point of view of the growers, then, the legal bushes *deserve* to be axed – to allow work to go ahead on the profit-making, illicit side.

It would be mistaken, however, to view the impending takeover of large sections of the Andean economies by deregulated, informal activity as an unmixed blessing. It suffers from many of the defects that free-trade systems have evidenced throughout history – notably, the fact that capital is free to act without any form of social and political constraint. The Andean states, whose national institutions have rarely been noted for their stability and continuity, risk becoming increasingly less viable as territorial entities the more their economies become part of a global black market spearheaded by the illicit drugs trade. It is for this reason that to speak of a 'national bourgeoisie' in the cocaine-producing countries is largely misleading, being based on an idea of national economies existing in relative isolation from each other. The cocaine economy is truly transnational, its mix of local and cosmopolitan elements being a function of the particular geographical settings of each stage of production rather than of clearly defined national interest groups. While a few trafficking syndicates do have a restricted geographical origin – Medellín in Colombia, Húanuco/Tingo Maria in Peru, Santa Cruz and Cochabamba in Bolivia – which can provide an ethnic esprit de corps similar to that of the Corsicans or Sicilians, most are nevertheless driven to employ chemists, pilots, 'enforcers', distributors, lawyers and financial advisers of the most diverse origins.

The transnational nature of the cocaine economy becomes even clearer if one turns from the subject of personnel to that of capital accumulation. At a time when exchange controls were lax and local markets offered a better rate of return than the world's leading financial centres, it was profitable to invest cocaine-derived capital within Latin America itself. As the economies of the region began to wind down and their financial markets became less profitable and more tightly controlled, much of this money migrated in search of better opportunities. What had previously been a reasonably safe bet, direct investment in the United States, found itself precluded by the threat of confiscation. The off-shore El Dorado thus remained the only viable alternative.

The various Caribbean tax havens have, in their time, provided useful outlets for this money, though two of the principal ones – The Bahamas and the Caymans – have under US pressure begun asking too many questions. If only for this reason, Panama – 'off shore' only in name, since it is geographically a part of the mainland – currently appears to be leading the field. Other factors contributing to this include its central location in terms of the region's air routes, the fact that it shares the Spanish language with many of its leading customers and the strength of its international banking sector, which has grown up since 1970 as the result of totally 'liberal' fiscal policies. Political stability, too, is provided by US forces in the Canal Zone and by a local government run by the National Guard, a police and military organization with an unsavoury human rights record.

Strategically, Panama is important to the US, which may explain the lack of official pressure from Washington regarding its money-laundering activities, despite several well-documented cases of corruption in the National Guard. It also uses the US dollar as its national currency, and by 1982 was returning over a billion dollars annually to the US Federal Reserve, repeating the prowess of Florida in the 1970s. In this way, it is a model for the denationalized, redollarized economies which are beginning to emerge through Latin America as local currencies collapse under the effects of hyperinflation.

This co-opting or recuperation of the profits of the informal and illicit sector proceeds through other mechanisms as well. Panama's banking business has been developed not through the system of 'brass-plate' private banks employed on the Caribbean islands, but through the creation of profitable opportunities for local branches of the world's leading commercial banks. In a system of double cover to their investors, these banks offer secret accounts to local companies which are allowed to have anonymous ownership and are free to move any amount of money in or out of Panama.

In short, Panama offers a tailor-made service to 'flight capital' of any origin; it would be impossible to assess how much of this originates in the illicit drugs trade. Its anomalous position – within the dollar zone in currency terms, outside it in terms of legal constraints – permits the growth of a capital sector which can offer considerable security and a generous return on investment. In the context of stagnant local economies, there is clearly a growing incentive for 'national capital' from the cocaine-producing states to internationalize itself in Panama. This would explain why the political impact of the 'emerging class' of blackmarket capitalists has not yet been commensurate with their growing economic weight. Thus the main question is not whether 'new money' from the illicit drugs trade will overtly take over the apparatus of Latin American states – a move that would not be in their interests – but whether this off-shore focus of the dollar economy may ever grow to the point of producing a political threat to the hegemony of Washington.

Certain investigators in the US Treasury appear to be taking this possibility seriously, at least if we are to take at face value their rhetoric about the drug-dealing 'scum growing on our society'. It would, however, be possible to argue quite the reverse, since the influx of narcodollars into Panama cannot, in the absence of sufficient investment possibilities in that country itself, remain there indefinitely. The search for profits may therefore ultimately draw cocaine money into ventures which, directly or indirectly, are designed to service the US budget deficit – part of which can be traced to the growing expenditure of Washington's 'war on drugs'.

A comparable circular logic underlies the wider impact which the illicit drugs trade is having in Latin America, and not only in those areas directly concerned with producing and shipping cannabis and cocaine. The export economies of Latin America have traditionally serviced their debt by maintaining large export surpluses, which have served to remit the earnings of capital back to the core states of the industrial West. However, with spiralling interest rates and the currently depressed value of traditional commodity exports, this balance has become increasingly difficult to maintain. It is clear, therefore, that the 'invisible' payments represented by cocaine exports and narcodollar deposits have – in the peculiar historical circumstances of the 1980s – played a principal role in taking up the slack.

It is not adequate, however, to maintain a simple two-way model of trade: cocaine moving in one direction, industrial goods in the other, the whole mediated through the use of blackmarket dollars. Latin America is not about to return to a colonial form of insertion in the world economy. The trading system ushered in by the cocaine cycle is triangular and represents an outgrowth of the type of internal colonialism which was characteristic of the preceding phase of industrialization. In this system, raw materials have been traded to the metropolitan powers, who in turn have exported capital to industrial enclaves in the developing world, which manufacture the goods that are used to supply the producers of raw materials. Though this scheme did generate a small amount of trade between the Latin American nations themselves, most countries remained tied to a partnership with their primary markets in the developed world, with the result that two points of the trading triangle – commodity production and enclave industry – occurred within single states. The variant introduced by the cocaine business has been the breakdown of international borders, the result of the extreme fluidity of a trading pattern which must of necessity be organized to transpose customs and tariff barriers. In view of the tremendous investment in anti-drugs customs enforcement, this development is not without its dose of irony.

Coca and cocaine production may remain concentrated in Peru, Bolivia and Colombia, but it shows a capacity for easy expansion into neighbouring areas of Brazil, Ecuador, Venezuela and Argentina and to more distant locations such as Paraguay or Mexico – not to mention Hawaii, which is already growing coca, and Florida and California, both of which share a capacity to refine cocaine hydrochloride out of smuggled cocaine base. The industrial enclaves that produce goods for the main coca-producing areas may be situated in local centres, such as Lima, Bogotá, Cali, Medellín – but equally, they may be located across international boundaries: in São Paulo, Buenos Aires and Manaus, or (through the free-trade zones in Paraguay and Panama) as far as Hong Kong and Taiwan. One look round a contraband stall in Bolivia can show the truly global extent of the commercial attraction exerted by cocaine earnings.

Even the apex of the triangle, traditionally located in the markets of the highly capitalized nations of Europe and North America, is becoming decentralized. A great deal of cocaine is consumed in the major cities of Latin America itself and thus it is impossible to continue giving credence to the DEA-promoted view of the economics of this drug – its little map with arrows showing the flow of the drug from leaf to street, and its inherent assumption that the US market is the ultimate destination, the major prize. Consuming centres have multiplied, production has become subject to the whims of an unregulated marketplace, processing and smuggling has diversified into a complex hierarchy of roles.

Towards legalization?

All the available evidence points to the coexistence of two very different strategies for the investment of capital accumulated in the cocaine enterprise. The first of these, and to date the most important, has been to retain funds in off-shore centres, where they add to the already swollen mass of speculative money on the world's financial markets. Should the entrepreneurs of the drugs trade be content with maintaining the role of an off-shore rentier class and enjoying a parasitic relationship with the major Western economies, the threat posed by their holdings can no doubt be absorbed without traumatizing the system.

But what if cocaine money were to realize the promise of a Carlos Lehder in Colombia, or of a Roberto Súarez in Bolivia? While hardly embracing a libertarian world view, such figures have nonetheless raised the possibility of a new, continent-wide, transnational bourgeoisie emerging from the cocaine trade, one with a vociferously anti-imperialist and anti-American position. Are their statements no more than smokescreens, or do they mean what they say?

Were they to put their money where their mouth is – investing their gains not just in the sort of populist showpiece projects which they have funded in the past, but in a serious and thoroughgoing penetration of local agriculture, commerce and industry – it is conceivable that they could reach the point of mounting an effective challenge to the stranglehold of foreign capital. Not, perhaps, through the expedient of actually buying out the multinationals' local subsidiaries, but instead by setting up rival concerns in the informal sector and using them effectively to destroy the formers' markets.

Such a scenario would be far more alarming to the major powers than any amount of illicit cocaine smuggling, and for this reason, its eventual emergence could provide a major motive for these powers to reconsider their intractable position on the legalization of coca and coca-derived products. In a legitimate market, the cocaine economy could be cut down to size: its profit margin reduced, overproduction encouraged to keep down raw material prices, and processing monopolized by large concerns with a firm control of market outlets. In short, coca could be induced to follow in the tradition established by coffee, sugar, cocoa, tobacco – the tradition of Third World dependency and metropolitan domination.

At least in the short term, however, this possibility does not appear very likely. Furthermore, it is clear that the current climate of repression – which forces down prices to the peasant producer and keeps them high for the consumer – works largely to the benefit of the cocaine-based entrepreneurial class, even if it occasionally causes the odd individual to suffer certain losses. For this reason, one obviously cannot take at face value the attempts of local governments to 'declare total war' on the cocaine trade, since such campaigns often respond to a barely concealed need to revitalize the blackmarket.

There are, however, a number of other forces tending towards the emergence of a strong pro-legalization lobby in the producing countries. A recent trend towards the location of final-stage cocaine-refining laboratories within the United States has been given a good deal of attention in the Latin American press – legalization could conceivably be proposed by local governments to counter this tendency, as industrial production is clearly cheaper nearer to the source of raw materials and cheap labour. Growing social unrest and the powerlessness of the state in the face of an effective takeover of local activity by the informal economy, could also produce a response (seriously entertained by economists in Peru, for example) of officializing the cocaine sector and absorbing its money-making capacity into the taxable, regulated, unionized economic world.

Last but not least, the purely financial rewards of legitimate cocaine exports could finally tip the balance, particularly in the context of the more bankrupt state economies of the Central Andes. In January 1985, the head of Bolivia's drug squad for the first time voiced public dismay at the DEA's insistence that all seized stocks of cocaine should be destroyed. Speaking at an official function where 166 kilos were about to be burned, Colonel Carlos Fernández pointed out:

> The destruction of this drug is a blow to Bolivia's economy, if you consider what it's worth in these days when our country is plunged into misery and one of the worst crises of its history. I think that the international organs of drug repression, or some interested nation, should buy the drug from us.

The colonel has also demanded a reform of the law which requires the incineration of seized cocaine. Should his idea catch on, the sale of cocaine by local governments to the major powers – to be equitable, this would have to be at current blackmarket prices – might provide a first step towards the ultimate legalization of the trade. For this reason alone, the DEA is unlikely to go along with the idea. The aim of international narcotics prohibition policy is hardly to encourage bankrupt states to boost illicit drug production, safe in the knowledge that the US Treasury will buy up a regular quota . . .

The basic weakness of all economic arguments in favour of legalization is that such a move would effectively undermine the extremely high profit margins currently enjoyed by the trade. It is most unlikely, therefore, that the cocaine entrepreneurs will ever countenance the idea. Indeed, it seems more probable that legalization would be introduced by those legitimate capital interests seeking to undermine the competition of the illicit market. That they do not proceed on these lines is evidence of their strong ideological commitment to stamping out illegal drug use – if not by overt repression (which has manifestly failed), at least by attempting to make individual drugs appear 'unfashionable'.

A backlash against cocaine has already been observable for some years in the United States; is there any possibility of the market declining into insignificance? On present evidence, this seems highly unlikely – for every media personality who gives up the drug, a hundred suburbanites take his or her place. The American market may be saturated, but new markets are booming in Europe and the more affluent areas of Latin America itself. Particularly through the expansion of cocaine base consumption, the drug is rapidly losing its elitist image and is becoming accessible to a vast mass of consumers of every social class.

This inevitably leads on to a consideration of the semiotics of the coca and cocaine markets. Coca chewing is eminently practical, but its image is backward and primitive – essentially *boring*, in the terms of urban society. (It will take a serious appraisal of the plant by Western practitioners of alternative medicine for the use of coca to spread beyond its present restricted range in South America.) The consumption of cocaine in base or hydrochloride form is much less practical – there are, in fact, cheaper and more efficient stimulants (amphetamine sulphate), as well as more saluburious alternatives (the various caffeinated beverages). All forms of cocaine, however, share a pronounced component of image-identification: *cool*, and somewhat upmarket, in the case of toot; *intense*, and rather downmarket, in the use of base.

Medical opinion on the harmfulness of cocaine use is divided, but it is almost unanimous in defending the traditional use of coca, which has been the object of several thorough studies undertaken in the indigenous context. What is evident, in the desire to tar coca with the same brush as cocaine, is an extraordinary ideological commitment to destroying a centuries-old custom shared by millions of healthy individuals, in the interests of reducing the availability of raw material for the production of cocaine. Such a strategy neglects the fact that once a social habit exists, it will always find ways of being supplied, no matter what the obstacles. Nevertheless, despite the veiled criticism of several other leading Western states (viz. McNicoll[26]), the US continues to push for the reduction of supply and the victimization of coca producers, rather than address itself to the more prickly question of reducing its own demand and educating its population to an adequate respect for the drug. This ideological commitment to compounding the cocaine problem with the destruction of the only really healthy and viable alternative, coca chewing, is made perfectly evident in the following words from the 1985 Congressional report:

> The Committee could then begin developing
> appropriate programs to gradually eliminate coca
> chewing in Bolivia by December 1989 . . . The
> chewing of coca leaf is a primitive, antiquated,
> debilitating practice, harmful to the individual and
> the public health and has considerable genocidal
> overtones.[27]

Such discourse is not scientific in any sense. It is no more than the propaganda of power – a terrorist discourse. It seeks to deny debate, to ignore the voice of users and producers. It seems hard to avoid the conclusion that what is being sought is the perpetuation and further escalation of the present alarming trends with all their ugly ramifications of selective victimization, distortion of the local economies and destruction of traditional practices.

The fact, however, that the discourse of drug repression is dressed up in scientific terms, rather than assuming its authoritarian character without any attempt at disguise, is also evidence of its weakness. The interminable production of pseudomedical anti-drug literature, achieved through the outright purchase of large sections of the research establishment, illustrates the weakness of official scientism: its need for legitimation. Hence also its obsessive manipulation of the communications media, its need to circumscribe the terms of the debate to issues amenable to control.

A recognition of this situation is one of the few positive signals to emerge from the chaos of present anti-drugs policies. For it offers the possibility of an argument in favour of legalization which is not couched in terms of the economic contradictions generated by the illicit trade, but in those of the medical and scientific discourse itself: the need to minimize any eventual harm resulting from the indiscriminate use of drug substances. For if one is to take seriously the argument that policy should be directed at minimizing such harm, one must start with the recognition that not all drug use is necessarily harmful, and that precedents do exist – in exotic cultures, certainly, but also in our own society – which are already pointing to ways out of the long night of repression and prohibition.

NOTES

Merchants of Death *v.* Junkie Babies

1. Panorama, 'Men of Honour', BBC TV, 1 April 1985.

1. Serious Business

Bad Moon Rising

1. National Narcotics Intelligence Consumers Committee, *The Supply of Drugs to the US Illicit Market from Foreign and Domestic Sources in 1978*, Washington: US Government Printing Office, 1980, pp.5–7.
2. *Ibid.*, p.11.
3. R. Hartnoll and R. Lewis, 'The Illicit Heroin Market in Britain, Towards a Preliminary Estimate of National Demand', ms., 1984.
4. R. Lewis, 'Sotto Un'Altro Vulcano, Interim Report on the Markets in Heroin and Cocaine in the Neapolitan Region', ms., 1985.
5. J.T. Maher, *Opium and Its Derivatives*, Washington: US Government Printing Office, 1980.
6. R. Lewis, 'The Illicit Traffic in Heroin', *Druglink*, 19, 1984, pp.7–14; and *Far Eastern Economic Review*, 4 August 1983.
7. UN Commission on Narcotic Drugs, *Review of the Illicit Traffic: Report by the Secretary-General*, UN, Vienna, 1985;

and UN Commission on Narcotic Drugs, *Report of the United Nations Fund for Drug Abuse Control*, 1984, UN, Vienna, 1985.

8. UN Commission on Narcotic Drugs, *Review of the Illicit Traffic: Report by the Secretary General*, UN, Vienna, 1985.

9. UN Commission on Narcotic Drugs, *Situation and Trends in Drug Abuse and the Illicit Traffic*, UN, Vienna, 1985.

10. UN Commission on Narcotic Drugs, *Report of the 14th Session of the Sub-Commission on Illicit Drug Traffic and Related Matters in the Near and Middle East*, UN, Vienna, 1983.

11. International Narcotics Control Board, Report, UN, Vienna, 1983.

12. G. Arrighi, 'A Crisis in Hegemony' in S. Amin, *et al.*, *Dynamics of Global Crisis*, London: Macmillan, 1982, p.77.

13. S. Amin, *et al.*, *Dynamics of Global Crisis*, London: Macmillan, 1982, p.229.

14. A.W. McCoy, *The Politics of Heroin in Southeast Asia*, New York: Harper & Row, 1972.

15. US Congressional Select Committee on Narcotics Abuse and Control, *Annual Report, 1984*, Washington: US Government Printing Office, 1985.

16. Royal Canadian Mounted Police, *National Drug Intelligence Estimates, 1983*, 1984.

17. US Congressional Select Committee on Narcotics Abuse and Control, *op. cit.*

18. S. Yurick, 'The Political Economy of Junk', *Monthly Review*, December 1970.

19. A. Gunder Frank, *Dependent Accumulation and Underdevelopment*, London: Macmillan, 1978, p.18.

20. W.J. Chambliss, 'The Political Economy of Smack: Opiates, Capitalism and Law', in R.J. Simon (ed.), *Research in Law and Sociology*, Greenwich, Conn: JAI Press, 1978, pp.115–41.

21. US Congressional Select Committee on Narcotic Abuse and Control, *op. cit.*
22. S. Mugford, 'Some Political and Economic Features of the Drug Trade', in G. Wardlaw (ed.), *Drug Trade and Drug Use*, Canberra: AFADD, 1982.

Whatever Happened to the French Connection?

1. L.R. Simmons and A.A. Said, (eds.), *Drugs, Politics and Diplomacy*, London: Sage, 1974; and C. Lamour and M. Lamberti, *The Second Opium War*, London: Allen Lane, 1974.
2. A. Jaubert, *Dossier D Comme Drogues*, Paris: Alain Moreau, 1975; P. Galante and L. Sapin, *The Marseilles Mafia*, London: W.H. Allen, 1982; and A.W. McCoy *et al.*, *The Politics of Heroin in Southeast Asia*, New York: Harper, 1973.
3. A.W. McCoy, *ibid.*; and *Newsday* editors, *The Heroin Trail*, London: Souvenir Press, 1974.
4. A. Jaubert, *op. cit.*
5. P. Galante and L. Sapin, *op. cit.*
6. J. Sarazin, *Dossier M Comme Milieu*, Paris: Alain Moreau, 1977.
7. R. Berdin, *Codename Richard*, London: New English Library, 1976; and P. Galante and L. Sapin, *op. cit.*
8. M. Auger, *The Heroin Triangle*, London: Methuen, 1978; and *Libération*, 16 April 1976.
9. *La Repubblica*, 'Dossier Mafia', 3 October 1984.
10. *Drug Enforcement*, (1973), I, pp.10–15.
11. R. Berdin, *op. cit.*; and *Daily Telegraph Magazine*, 17 August 1982.
12. *Newsday* editors, *op. cit.*
13. A. Jaubert, *op. cit.*; and J. Hougan, *Spooks, The Private Use of Secret Agents*. London: W.H. Allen, 1979.
14. A. Jaubert, *op. cit.*
15. M. Pelletier, *Rapport de la mission d'étude sur l'ensemble des problèmes de la drogue*, Paris: La Documentation Française, 1978.

16. A. Jaubert, *op.cit.*; P. Galante and L. Sapin, *op.cit.*; and *Washington Post*, 24 May 1972.

17. A.W. McCoy *et al.*, *op.cit.*

18. A. Jaubert *op.cit.*; and J. Sarazin, *op.cit.*

19. *Nouvel Observateur*, 22 November 1971.

20. *Newsday* editors, *op.cit.*

21. *Agence France Presse*, 19 September 1972.

22. *Newsday* editors, *op.cit.*

23. J. Derogy and J-M. Pontaut, *Enquête sur les Mystères de Marseilles*, Paris: Robert Lafont, 1984; and *Rapport de la Commission d'Enquête sur les activités du Service d'Action Civique*, Paris: Alain Moreau, 1982, two volumes.

24. *Libération*, April 1978, *passim*.

25. M. Auger, *op.cit.*; and A. Laville, *Le Juge Michel*, Paris: Presse de la Cité, 1982.

26. A. Laville, *op.cit.*; and J. Derogy and J-M. Pontaut, *op.cit.*

27. N. Lewis, *The Honoured Society*, London: Eland, 1984.

28. P. Arlacchi, *et al.*, *Morte di un Generale*, Milan: Mondadori, 1982.

29. M. Cimino, in N. Lewis, *The Honoured Society*, London: Eland, 1984.

30. N. Dalla Chiesa, *Delitto Imperfetto*, Milan: Mondadori, 1984.

31. *La Repubblica*, *op. cit.*, and R. Minna, *Breve Storia della Mafia*, Rome: Riuniti, 1984.

Users, Dealers and Villains

1. T.H. Bewley, I.P. James, and T. Mahon 'Evaluation of the Effectiveness of Prescribing Clinics for Narcotic Addicts in the United Kingdom' in C.J.D. Zarafonetis (ed.), *Drug Abuse*, Philadelphia: Lee & Febiger, 1972, pp.73–92.

2. G.V. Stimson and E. Oppenheimer, *Heroin Addiction – Treatment and Control in Britain* London: Tavistock, 1982; and R.L. Hartnoll and M.C. Mitcheson, 'Evaluation of Heroin Maintenance in Controlled Trial', *Archive of General*

Psychiatry, 37, 1980, pp.877–84.

3. Her Majesty's Government, *Report to the United Nations on the Working of the International Treaties on Narcotic Drugs in the United Kingdom of Great Britain and Northern Ireland*, 1976.

4. Release, *Newsrelease*, October–December 1977.

5. D. Clark, 'Smack in the Capital', *Time Out*, 53, 1980, pp.11–13.

6. R.L. Hartnoll, R.J. Lewis and S. Bryer, 'Recent Trends in Drug Use in Britain', *Druglink*, 19, 1984, pp.22–4.

7. World in Action, 'The Heroin Barons' (transcript), Granada Television, 13 June 1983.

8. Her Majesty's Government, *Report to the United Nations on the Working of the International Treaties on Narcotic Drugs in the United Kingdom of Great Britain and Northern Ireland*, 1980; Her Majesty's Government, *Report to the United Nations on the Working of the International Treaties on Narcotic Drugs in the United Kingdom of Great Britain and Northern Ireland*, 1981; Her Majesty's Government, *Report to the United Nations on the Working of the International Treaties on Narcotic Drugs in the United Kingdom of Great Britain and Northern Ireland*, 1982; and Her Majesty's Customs and Excise, 'Record Customs Heroin Seizures', *Press Notice* 799, 5 January 1983.

9. M. Ashton, 'What's Happening with Heroin?' *Druglink*, 17, 1982 1–5.

10. G.F. Brown and L.R. Silverman, *The Retail Price of Heroin, Estimations and Applications*, Washington: Drug Abuse Council, 1973; M.H. Moore, *Buy and Bust, the Effective Regulation of an Illicit Market in Heroin*, Lexington, Mass: Lexington, 1977; and E. Preble and J.J. Casey, 'Taking Care of Business. The Heroin User's Life on the Street', *International Journal of the Addictions*, 4, 1969, pp. 1–24.

11. P. Arlacchi, *Mafia Imprenditrice*, Bologna: Il Mulino, 1983; and P.J. Goldstein *et al.*, 'The Marketing of Street

Heroin in New York City', *Journal of Drug Issues*, 14, 3, 1984, pp.533–66.

12. Her Majesty's Government, 1980, *op.cit.*; Her Majesty's Government, 1982, *op.cit*; and Under-Secretary of State for Home Affairs, *Hansard*, 12 July 1984.

13. Department of Employment, 'General Index of Retail Prices: All Items', *Employment Gazette*, January 1981, S 58, 6.4; and Department of Employment, 'General Index of Retail Prices: All Items', *Employment Gazette*, January 1984, S 58, 6.4.

14. R. Lewis *et al.*, 'Scoring Smack, The Illicit Heroin Market in London, 1980–83', *British Journal of Addiction*, September 1985; and UN Commission on Narcotic Drugs, *Review of the Illicit Traffic: Report by the Secretary-General*, UN, Vienna, 1985.

15. M.H. Moore, *op.cit.*; and S. Rottenberg, 'The Clandestine Distribution of Heroin', *Journal of Political Economy*, 76, 1968, pp.78–90.

16. UN Commission on Narcotic Drugs, *op.cit.*

Note for fuller details of the work in this chapter see R. Lewis *et al.*, 'Scoring, Smack, The Illicit Heroin Market in London, 1980–83', *British Journal of Addiction*, September 1985.

2. The Cost of Lacoste

1.R. Elms, *The Face*, No. 51, 1984.

2. P. Willis, *Profane Culture*, London: Routledge & Kegan Paul, 1978.

Further reading
G. Clarke, *Defending Ski-Jumpers: A Critique of Theories of Youth Subcultures*, Centre for Contemporary Cultural Studies University of Birmingham, 1982.

S. Hall, *The Hippies: an American Moment*, CCCS, 1968.

S. Hall and T. Jefferson, *Resistance through Rituals*, London: Hutchinson, 1976.

P. Marsh, *et al. The Rules of Disorder*, London: Routledge &
Kegan Paul, 1978.
G. Mungham, *Working-Class Youth Culture*, London:
Routledge & Kegan Paul, 1976.
T. Veblen, *The Theory of the Leisure Class*, London: George
Allen & Unwin, 1970.

3. Love Seeds and Cash Crops

1. Select Committee on Narcotics Abuse and Control, *Annual
Report to Congress, 1984*, Washington: US Government
Printing Office, 1985.
2. United Nations ECOSOC Commission on Narcotic Drugs:
various reports.
3. Wayne Greenhaw, *Flying High*, New York: Dodd, Mead,
1984.
4. NORML 1984 Marijuana Crop Report, Washington DC.
5. NORML, 'Camp Program Enjoined', *The Leaflet*,
February 1985.
6. B. du Toit, *Cannabis in Africa*, Rotterdam: A.A. Balkema,
1980.
7. J. Gené, 'Les Américains aboient, le trafic passe',
Libération, 19/20 January 1985.
8. D. Leigh, *High Time*, London: Heinemann, 1984.

Further reading
D. Aitken and T. Mikuriya, 'The Forgotten Medicine', *The
Ecologist*, October, November 1980.
L. Barrett, *The Rastafarians*, London and Jamaica:
Heinemann Sangsters, 1977.
W. Buckley, 'Legalize Dope', *Washington Post*, April 1985.
H. Campbell, 'Rastafari, Culture of Resistance', *Race and
Class*, XXII, 1, 1980.
H. de Monfreid, *La Crosière du Hachich*, London:
MacDonald & Janes, 1935.

C. Dickey, 'Ganja Buoys Jamaica', *Washington Post*, 10 November 1980.

R. Evans and R. Pisani, *The Regulation and Taxation of Cannabis Commerce*, Philadelphia: ILDC, 1982.

S. Flynn and Yeates, *Smack*, Dublin: Gill and Macmillan 1985.

D. Hallenstein, 'A Town They Call Hashville', *Sunday Times*, 11 November 1984.

B. Hilliard, 'Why Not Let The Grass Grow?' *Police Review*, 5 April 1985 and 12 April 1985.

P. Hughes *et al.*, 'Extent of Drug Abuse: An International Review', *World Health Statistics Quarterly*, 36, 1983.

R. Lee, *Operation Julie*, London: W.H. Allen, 1978.

F. Logan, *Cannabis. Options For Control*. Sunbury: Quartermaine, 1979.

T. Malyon, 'Bibles in the Ganja Fields', *Home Grown*, Winter 1983.

T. Malyon, 'Church Corners Cannabis Market', *New Statesman*, 30 May 1980.

T. Malyon, 'Just Another Cash Crop?', *The Ecologist*, October/ November 1980.

T. Malyon and A. Henman, 'No Marijuana, Plenty of Hemp', *New Scientist*, 13 November 1980.

H. Messick, *Of Grass and Snow*, New Jersey: Prentice-Hall, 1979.

J. Michell, 'Grow Hemp . . . Or Else . . .', *The Ecologist*, October/ November 1980.

J. Owens, *Dread*, Kingston: Sangsters.

M. Royko, 'Legal Marijuana – A Pot of Gold', *Chicago Tribune*, 3 March 1985.

V. Rubin and L. Comitas, *Ganja in Jamaica*, New York: Anchor Books, 1976.

Jack Shafer, 'War Can't Be Won; It's Time We Gave Up', *USA Today*, February 1985.

S. Tendler and D. May, *The Brotherhood of Eternal Love*, London: Granada 1984.

4. Psychotropics, Passivity and the Pharmaceutical Industry

1. Ian Gough, *The Political Economy of the Welfare State*, London: Macmillan, 1979.
2. A. Oakley, *Subject Women*, London: Fontana, 1981.
3. Lesley Doyal, with Imogen Pennell, *The Political Economy of Health*, London: Pluto Press, 1979.
4. Nancy Chodorow, *The Reproduction of Mothering: Psychoanalysis and the Sociology of Gender*, Berkeley: University of California Press, 1978.
5. I. Bruegel, 'Women as a Reserve Army of Labour: a Note on Recent British Experience' in E. Whitelegg *et al.* (eds.), *The Changing Experience of Women*, London: Open University Press, 1982.
6. G.W. Brown and T. Harris, *Social Origins of Depression: A Study of Psychiatric Disorder in Women*, London: Tavistock, 1978.
7. G.B. Hill, 'The Expectations of Being Admitted to a Mental Hospital in DHSS Psychiatric Hospitals in England and Wales', in *Patient Statistics from the Mental Health Enquiry, 1970*, London: HMSO, 1972.
8. S. Lipshitz, 'Women and Psychiatry' in J. Chetwynd and O. Hartnet (eds.), *The Sex Role System*, London: Routledge and Kegan Paul, 1978 pp.93–108.
9. C. Offe, 'Advanced Capitalism and the Welfare State', *Politics and Society*, 2, 1972, pp.479–89.
10. T. Malyon, 'The Production and Consumption of Illegal Drugs', *Behind the News*, 1984, pp.131–7.
11. S. Shaw, 'The Causes of Increasing Drinking Problems amongst Women in Camberwell' Council on Alcoholism, *Women and Alcohol*, London: Tavistock, 1980.
12. K. Brunn, (ed.), *Alcohol Control Policies in the United Kingdom*, Stockholm: Sociologiska Instituten, 1982.
13. J. Cavanagh and F. Clairmonte, *Alcoholic Beverages, Dimensions of Corporate Power*, Geneva: World Health

Organization: 1983.

14. S. Otto, 'Women, Alcohol and Social Control', in B. Hunter and G. Williams (eds.), *Controlling Women: the Normal and the Deviant*, London: Croom Helm, 1981 pp.154–67.

15. A. Maynard and R. McDonnell, 'The Cost of Alcohol Misuse', *British Journal of Addiction* (forthcoming).

16. J. White, *Women and Alcohol*, unpublished paper presented at two-day conference, Left Alive, in London 2,3,4 November 1984.

17. OHE, *Office of Health Economics Compendium of Health Statistics*, 5th Edition, London: OHE, 1984.

18. *Lancet*, Vol. 12, 1978, p.946.

19. R. Lacey, 'Prescriptions – What Price Official Secrecy?' *Open Mind*, No. 9, 1984, p.13.

20. A. Clare, 'Psychotropic Drug Use in General Practice' in G. Tognoni, C. Bellantuono and M. Lader (eds.), *Epidemiological Impact of Psychotropic Drugs*, Amsterdam: Elsevier/North Holland Biomedical Press, 1981, pp.189–201.

21. ISDD, *Prevalence of Psychotropic Drug Taking Amongst Women in the UK*, London: ISDD, 1980.

22. ISDD, *Surveys and Statistics on Drug Taking in Britain*, London: ISDD, 1984.

23. MIND, National Association for Mental Health, 'What the Patient Ought to Know But Is Not Told: the True Price of Tranquillity', Press release, London: Mind, National Association Mental Health, 1 February 1984.

24. P. Parish, 'The Prescribing of Psychotropic Drugs in General Practice', *The Journal of the Royal College of General Practitioners*, Supplement No. 4, 1971, 21, 92.

25. M. Lader, 'Benzodiazepines – the Opium of the Masses?', *Neuroscience*, Vol. 3, 1978, pp.159–65.

26. A. Jamieson, A. Glanz and S. MacGregor, *Dealing with Drug Misuse: Crisis Intervention in the City*, London: Tavistock, 1984.

27. P. Williams, 'Recent Trends in the Prescribing of

Psychotropic Drugs', *Health Trends*, 12, 1980, pp.6–7.
28. OHE, 'Medicines and the Quality of Life', *OHE Briefing*, No. 19, 1982.
29. M. Lader, 'Dependence on Benzodiazepines', *Journal of Clinical Psychiatry*, 44, 4, 1983, pp.121–7.
30. Committee on the Review of Medicine, 'Systematic Review of the Benzodiazepines', *British Medical Journal*, 29 March 1980, pp.910–2.
31. M. Lader, 'Introduction' in C. Haddon, *Women and Tranquillizers*, London: Sheldon Press, 1984.
32. Release, *Trouble with Tranquillizers*, London: Release, 1982.
33. Joy Melville, *The Tranquillizer Trap*, London: Fontana, 1984.
34. G.V. Stimson, 'The Message of Psychotropic Drug Ads', *Journal of Communication*, 25, 3, 1975, pp.153–60.
35. K. Nairne and G. Smith, *Dealing with Depression*, London: The Women's Press, 1984.
36. M. Barrett and H. Roberts, 'Doctors and their Patients: The Social Control of Women in General Practice', in C. Smart and B. Smart (eds), *Women, Sexuality and Social Control*, London: Routledge & Kegan Paul, 1978.
37. B. Ehrenreich and D. English, *Complaints and Disorders: The Sexual Politics of Sickness*, London: Compendium, 1974.
38. D. Harpwood, *Tea and Tranquillizers*, London: Virago Press, 1982.
39. Lyn Perry, author of *Women and Drug Use: an Unfeminine Dependency*, London: ISDD, 1979, provided valuable advice and support in the preparation of this chapter.

5. Cocaine Futures

1. James Dunkerley, *Rebellion in the Veins: Political Struggle in Bolivia 1952–82*, London: Verso, 1984, p. 308.
2. Jean-Pierre Gené, 'Mama Coca Papa Dollar', *Libération*, 17–19 January 1985.

3. Thomas Szasz, *Ceremonial Chemistry: The Ritual Persecution of Drugs, Addicts and Pushers*, Garden City, New York: Anchor Press/Doubleday, 1974.

4. William E. Carter *et al.*, *La Coca en Bolivia*, La Paz: UFLA/NIDA, 1980.

5. Anon, 'Crónica: La coca; sus productores, consumidores y la ley 22095', *Antropologia Andina*, No. 3, 1979, pp.89–99 (Cusco).

6. US Congress, *Annual Report for the Year 1984 of the Select Committee on Narcotics Abuse and Control*, Washington: US Government Printing Office, 1985, 17 p.130.

7. Jean-Pierre Gené, *op.cit.*

8. Henri Favre, 'Sentier lumineux et horizons obscurs', *Problèmes d'Amérique Latine*, No. 72, 1984, p.16 (Paris).

9. Anthony Henman, *Mama Coca*, Bogotá: El Ancora/La Oveja Negra, 1981. 'Antonil, *Mama Coca*, London: Hassle Free Press, 1979.

10. US Congress, *op.cit.*

11. Alvaro Camacho Guizado, 'Cocaína, Economía y Poder' in *Alternativa*, Nos. 200–202 1979, (Bogotá). *Droga, Corrupción y Poder: Marihuana y Cocaína en la Sociedad Colombiana*, Cali: CIDSE/Universidad del Valle, 1981.

12. ANIF (Asociación Nacional de Instituciones Financieras), *Marihuana: Legalización o Represión*, Bogotá: Biblioteca ANIF de Economia, 1979.

13. Henri Favre, *op.cit.*, p.24.

14. Philip Parkerson in Carter *et al.*, *op.cit.* Javier Albó 'Coripata: Sus Haciendas y su Historia', *Avances* (La Paz), no. 2, 1978.

15. José Blanes and Gonzalo Flores, *Campesino, Migrante y Colonizador: Reproducción de la Economía Familiar en el Chapare Tropical*, La Paz: Ediciones CERES, 1982.

16. Amado Canelas Orellana, and Juan Carlos Canelas Zannier, *Bolivia: Coca Cocaína*, Cochabamba: Los Amigos del Libro, 1983, p.226.

17. David Goodman and Michael Redclift, *From Peasant to*

Proletarian, Oxford: Basil Blackwell, 1981, p.109.

18. Freddy Artenga, Mauricio Mamani *et al.*, *Uso Tradicional de la Coca en Bolivia*, La Paz: Museo Nacional de Etnografía y Folklore, 1978.

19. René Bascopé Aspiazu, *La Veta Blanca: Coca y Cocaína en Bolivia*, La Paz: Ediciones Aquí, 1982. IEPALA, *Narcotráfico y Política: Militarismo y Mafia en Bolivia*, Madrid: IEPALA, 1982.

20. Carlos C. Cagliotti, 'Some Considerations about the Chewing of Coca Leaf in The Argentine Republic, in F.R. Jeri, (ed.), *Cocaine: 1980*, Lima: World Health Organization, 1980.

21. *Ibid.*

22. Anthony Henman and Oswaldo Pessoa, *Diamba Sarabamba*, São Paulo: Ground/Global, 1985.

23. UN, *Methods for the Eradication of Illicit Narcotic Crops*, Geneva: United Nations Narcotics Laboratory (MNAR/8/1979).

24. Geoffrey Kay, *Development and Underdevelopment: A Marxist Analysis*, London: Macmillan, 1975.

25. US Congress, *op.cit.*, p.17.

26. André McNicoll, *Drug Trafficking: A North-South Perspective*, Ottawa: The North-South Institute, 1983.

27. US Congress, *op.cit.* p.21.

INDEX

ADEPA (Cotton Producers Association), 154
Afghanistan, 9–11, 13, 15–16, 65, 88, 90
Africa, 18, 79
Aguilar, Judge Robert, 74
AID, 134, 145, 177
Ajaccio Junior Chamber of Commerce, 32
Alberti, Gerlando, 36
Algeria, 23, 32
Allende, Salvador, 66
Alliance for Progress, 157
Amazon, 99, 125, 128, 162–4, 168
America (North), 10, 17, 23–9, 31, 33–4, 38–9, 45, 51, 80, 119, 127, 129, 131, 133–4, 138–9, 149–50, 158–9, 161, 170, 181, 187
Amin, Samir 14
Amsterdam, 97, 99, 168
Andes, 148, 150, 153, 161–2, 164, 167, 172, 177–8, 185
Anglo-Indian government, 17
Antimafia Commission, 9

Arawak, 79
Argentina, 158–61, 174, 177, 182
Africa, 158
Arlacchi, Pino, 9
Armenia, 26
Asia, 33
Atlantic City, 97
Australia, 101
Aymara Indians, 146

Badalamenti, Gaetano, 38
Bahamas, 65, 76, 97, 131, 179
Baluchistan, 13
Bangladesh, 66
Bank of Jamaica, 65
Banzer, 156
Barclays Bank, 52
Bascopé Aspiazu, René, 154
Basildon, 50
Bay of Pigs, 64
Beirut, 29
Bekaa valley, 13, 87
Belize, 65, 69–71, 76, 86, 131, 157
Beni, 154–6

Betancur, Belisario, 132,
136–8, 142, 176
Binh Xuyen, 30–31
Bishop, Maurice, 70
Blanes, José, 150
Bogotá, 136, 168, 182
Bolivia, 116, 121, 124, 126,
131, 140, 143–7, 152–3,
155–6, 158–60, 163, 167,
170–1, 173–8, 182–2, 185,
188
Bonanno, 38
Bontade, 37–8
Bowie, David, 54
Brasilia, 162
Brazil, 119, 125, 128, 131–3,
139–40, 143, 151, 157,
161–3, 165–8, 174, 177,
182
Brazilian Federal Police,
163, 165–6
Briceõ, Eligio, 71
Britain, 5, 8–9, 13, 40–2,
45–6, 49, 53, 70, 71, 78–
9, 87, 89–93, 96–7,
103–7, 108–9, 115, 125,
158
British American Tobacco
(BAT), 111
British Broadcasting
Corporation (BBC), 88–9
Brodie, Alex, 89
Brotherhood of Eternal
Love, 63–4
Buckley, William, 100
Buenos Aires, 159–60, 182

Bureau of Narcotics and
Dangerous Drugs
(BNDD), 28
Burma, 10–11, 15
Burroughs, William, 5
Burrows, David, 76
Buscetta, Tommaso, 27

Cagliotti, Carlos, 161
Cali, 182
California, 69, 73–6, 119,
182
Camacho, Alvaro, 141–2
Camarena, Enrique, 133
Campaign Against
Marijuana Planting
(CAMP), 74–5
Campaign on the Use and
Restriction of Barbiturates
(CURB), 113
Campbell, Horace, 80
Canada, 16, 25, 78
Canelas, Juan Carlos, 150
Canelas Orellana, Amado,
150
Caquetá, 137, 164
Carbone, Bonaventre, 24, 30
Caribbean, 81, 84, 138, 179–
80, (Basin Initiative –
CBI), 69–70
Carter, William E., 126, 146
Castro, Fidel, 64, 83, 132
Catania, 37–8
Cayman Islands, 96, 98–9,
179
Central America, 68–71, 90

Central Drugs Intelligence
    Unit, 78
Channel Islands, 2
Chapare, 146–56, 168–9
Chihuahua, 85, 169
Chile, 66, 158–60
Chimoré, 149
China, 13, 17, 40, 102, 125
Chinnici, Judge Rocco, 39
Cholon, 30
Christian Democrat, 37, 39
CIA, 28, 31, 35, 66, 69, 90,
    131
Ciancimino, Vito, 39
Cochabamba, 118, 122, 145–
    6, 148, 151–4, 168–9, 171,
    175, 178
Colombia, 65, 69–70, 75–8,
    86, 91, 96, 131–2, 136–43,
    155, 156, 162–7, 170–1,
    176, 178, 182–3
Committee on the Review of
    Medicines, 114
Commonwealth, 2
Conteh, John, 52
Contras, 69
Coptic Church, 81–3
Cordillera Real, 147
Coripata, 147
Corleone, 37
Corr, Edwin, 124, 143
Corsica, 23, 25, 27, 29, 32,
    178
Costa Rica, 69
Cuba, 64, 83, 131
Cusack, John, 28–9

Cusco, 127
Customs and Excise, 49
Cyprus, 13

Dalla Chiesa, General, 35,
    37, 39
De Gaulle, Charles, 29, 32
De Quincey, Thomas, 40
d'Estaing, Giscard, 32
Delouette, Roger, 31
Denny, California, 74
Department of Employment,
    46
Deuxiéme Bureau, 31
Diem, President, 31
Doctor Martens, 54
Drugs Enforcement
    Administration (DEA),
    66–8, 70–4, 85–6,
    122–4, 127, 131, 133–4,
    136, 138, 140, 153–4,
    160–3, 166–70, 183,
    185–6
du Toit, Brian, 79
Dublin, 94
Dunkerley, James, 121
Dunne family, 94

East End, 52, 55
East India Company, 16
Ecuador, 157, 182
Egypt, 65, 88
El Salvador, 69–70
Elms, Richard, 53–4
England, 113
Esquivel, Manuel, 70

Europe, 5, 11–13, 16–17, 24, 28, 40–2, 46, 63, 72, 87–9, 95, 125–6, 187

Falcone, Judge Giovanni, 39
Far East, 24
Favre, Henri, 135, 143
Felixstowe, 8
Fernández, Colonel Carlos, 185
Fifth Republic, 32
First National Bank of Boston, 97
Flores, Gonzalo, 150
Florida, 82, 139, 179, 182
France, 23–36, 39
Francisci, Marcel, 25, 29
Front de Liberation Nationale (FLN), 32

Gairy, Eric, 80
Gambino, 37
Garcia Meza, 131, 140–1, 149, 152, 156
Gaullism, 23, 29–30, 32–5
Gené, J.P., 86, 135
Geneva Convention, 1925, 158
Genoa, 25
George III, 17
German occupation, 27
Gestapo, 30
Glastonbury, 103
Goldsack, James, 96
Goodman, David, 151

Gorbals, 52
Gould, David, 97
Gramsci, Antonio, 6
Granada TV, 106
Greco, 37
Greek dealers, 58
Greenhaw, Wayne, 68–9
Grenada, 80, 83
Guadalajara, 133
Guajira peninsula, 75, 136
Guatemala, 68–70
Guerini brothers, 24, 29

Hague Convention, 125
Harpwood, D., 116
Harris, Sydney, 100
Harvard Business School, 65
Hawaii, 73, 182
Heathrow, 95
Hell's Angels, 64
Henman, Anthony, 162
Hickling, Freddy, 80
Himalayas, 91
Hoffman La Roche, 112
Home Office, 8
Honduras, 65, 68–70, 131
Hong Kong, 13
Huallaga valley, 134
Húanaco, 178

Inca conquest, 158
India, 13, 65, 76, 79, 91, 96, 104
Indiana, 139
Indochina, 23–4, 30
Inland Revenue, 97

Institute for the Study of Drug Dependence (ISDD), 112
Institute of Development Studies, 80
International Monetary Fund (IMF), 82, 102, 177
International Narcotics Control Amendment (1983), 132
Interpol, 29, 154
Inzerillo, 37–8
Iran, 11, 13, 16, 41, 42, 47
Iraq, 13
Islamabad, 89
Israel, 88
Italy, 3, 9, 23–35, 34–5, 39

Jamaica, 63–5, 70, 76–85, 101–2, 131, 157
Javarí river, 167
Judge, Tony, 101
Jujuy, 158–60

Kabul, 15
Karachi, 16, 89
Kay, Geoffrey, 172
Kemp, Gary, 53
Kingston, Jamaica, 76–7, 80, 85
Krogh, Egil, 28
Kuomintang, 15
Kurdestan, 13

La Paz, 143, 146–7, 152, 156, 168, 175

Labay, André, 31
Lacoste, 54
Lader, M., 113
Lane, Patrick, 96–7
Lara Bonilla, Rodrigo, 136
Laos, 15
Latin America, 28, 30, 130, 132, 139, 140, 157, 161, 172, 178–183, 185, 187
Le Havre, 31
Lebanon, 13, 25, 63–5, 76, 87–8, 91, 103
Legalize Cannabis Campaign, 103, 105
Lehder, Carlos, 138, 183
Leigh, David, 96
Leticia, 164, 166
Levi's, 54
Lewis, Roger, 9, 46
Lima, Peru, 136, 168, 172, 177, 182
London, 7, 29, 40–3, 45, 47, 50–1, 57–8, 94, 101, 104, 169; (East), 60
Los Angeles, 41
Lucania, Salvatore (Charlie 'Lucky' Luciano), 24

Madrid, 38
Mafia, 3, 24–7, 33–9; (Interprovincial Commission), 38
Makú, 163
Manaus, 182
Manley, Michael, 70, 82–3, 102

Marcellin, Raymond, 32
Marks, Howard, 95–7
Marley, Bob, 80
Marseilles, 23–4, 26–8, 33–6
Marshall plan, 24
Marx, Karl, 9
McNicoll, A., 188
Medellín, 171, 178, 182
Mediterranean, 12, 23–4, 29, 33
Melville, Joy, 115
Mexico, 10, 13, 25, 33, 64, 70, 85–6, 133, 139, 157, 161, 177
Miami, 71, 81–3, 99, 137, 155
Michel, Judge Pierre, 35–6
Middle East, 11, 13
MIND, 113
Missick, Stafford, 71
Montalto, Judge Ciaccio, 39
Moore, Mark, 47–8
Morocco, 65, 103
Moser, Brian, 137
Movimiento Cívico Latino Nacional, 138
Mujahideen, 16, 90, 94

Naples,9, 25
National Health Service (NHS), 108–12, 114
National Institute of Drug Abuse (NIDA), 129
National Organization for the Reform of Marijuana Laws (NORML), 73
Nazi collaborators, 30

Near East, 11, 24
Nepal, 65, 66
New England, 18
New Jersey, 97
New Jewel Movement (NJM), 80
New South Wales, 101
New York, 3–4, 25–6, 45, 47, 96–7, 128, 168–9, 175
Newman, Sir Kenneth, 101
Nicaragua, 68–70, 131
Nigeria, 65
Nixon, Richard, 27, 132
Northwest Frontier, 11–13, 15, 102

Offe, C., 110
Old Bailey, 95
Oldham, Harold, 98–9
Organisation de L'Armée Secréte (DAS), 32
Organisation of American States, 161
Operation Chemcon, 140
Operation Hat Trick, 138
Operation X, 31
Oruro, 148

Pakistan, 9–13, 15–16, 42, 47, 49, 64–5, 88–91, 102
Palermo, 25–6, 35–8
Palermo, Judge Carlo, 39
Palestine Liberation Organization (PLO), 88

Panama, 137, 174, 179–82;
  (Canal Zone), 179;
  (National Guard); 179
Paraguay, 30, 131–2, 140,
  157, 174, 182
Paris, 24, 29
Parkerson, Peter, 146
Pathan, 10
Peking, 16
Pelletier Report, 30
Performance, 55–6
Peru, 126–7, 133–7, 143–5,
  156, 162–3, 166–7, 172,
  176–8, 185
Pessoa, Oswaldo, 162
Phalangists, 88
Philippines, 65, 68
Police Federation, 101
Pompidou, President, 32
Port Elizabeth, New Jersey,
  31
Potosí, 148, 152
Póvoa, Hugo, 166
Prescription Pricing
  Authority (PPA), 112
Price, George, 70
Provisional IRA, 96
Putumayo, 164

Quechua Indians, 146
Quillabamba, 127

Rangel Amendment (1972),
  132
Rastafarianism, 77, 79–82
Reagan, Ronald, 70

Red Sea, 128
Redclift, Michael, 151
Release, 115
Reuters, 37
Rich, Dawn, 81
Ricord, Auguste, 30
Rio de Janeiro, 163
Rio Negro, 163–5
Rizla cigarette papers, 106
Rock Against Racism, 52
Rolicheck, Judy, 74
Rosenthal, Ed, 73
Rottenberg, S., 48
Russia, 89–90

Saatchi and Saatchi, 56
Sabiani, Simon, 24
Saigon, 30–31
Salan, General Raoul, 31
Salesian mission, 165
Salta, 158–60
San Javier/Portachuelo, 155
San Pedro de Jujuy, 158
Sandinista, 69
Santa Cruz, 153–6, 168, 178
Santapaola, 38
Sáo Paulo, 163, 168, 182
Saunders, Norman, 71
Scotland, 95–6
Scythians, 102
Seaga, Edward, 65 83–5
Sendero Luminoso, 135, 166
Senegal, 65
Service d'Action Civique
  (SAC), 30, 32–3,
  35

Service de Documentation et de Contre-Espionage (SDECE), 31, 32, 34–5
Shan states, 10
Shanghai Commission, 125
Sheridan, Michael, 37
Shultz, George, 129, 131, 135
Sicily, 25, 27, 33, 35–8, 178
Sile government, 147
Siles Zuazo, 144, 152
Sindona, Michele, 39
Single Convention on Narcotic Drugs (1961), 157
Somoza, 69
South Africa, 79
South America, 30, 69, 71, 95, 120, 124, 126, 138–9, 140, 187
South Asia, 17
Southeast Asia, 11–13, 28, 32, 33, 35, 41, 47
Southwest Asia, 11–12, 38, 42, 49, 88
Spain, 132
Spanish Conquest, 126
Spatola, 37
Spirito, Franois, 24–5, 30
Sri Lanka, 65, 68
Star Island, 82–3
Stonehenge, 103
Stop The City, 52
Stroessner, General, 30, 131–2
Súarez, Roberto, 183
Surinam, 131
Swaziland, 65

Switzerland, 3
Syria, 13, 87–8, 159
Szasz, Thomas, 124

Taiwan, 182
Tefé, 164–5
Texas, 69
Thailand, 11, 13, 15–16, 47, 65
Tingo Maria, 127, 178
Tories, 56
Tosh, Peter, 89
Tukano, 163
Turkey, 11, 13, 25–6, 33, 35–6, 42
Turks and Caicos Islands, 71–2, 131
Turner, Carlton, 70
Turner, Christopher, 71

Union Corse, 27
United Kingdom, 6, 42, 45, 64, 78, 89–90, 92, 95, 106
United Nations, 46, 67, 89, 98, 159, 161; (Commission on Narcotic Drugs), 68; (Single Convention), 66
United States, 3, 9, 15–17, 23–8, 30, 34, 36, 38–40, 63, 65–75, 78, 81–90, 95, 97–100, 102, 110, 125–6, 128, 131–4, 136–40, 148, 151, 155, 157, 161, 163, 166, 169–71, 176–7, 179–81, 183, 185–6, 188; (Congressional Select

United States contd:
Committee), 67, 70, 73, 126,
 139, 188; (Customs), 82,
 133; (Federal Reserve),
 179; (Foreign Assistance
 Act), 69; (Information
 Agency) 123; (Senate
 Committee on
 Governmental Affairs), 98;
 (State Department), 70,
 132–4, 138, 156
Uyuni, 160

Vallegrande, 155
Valverde, Carlos, 154
Vaupés, 137, 165
Venezuela, 143, 161–2, 182
Venturi, Nick 25
Vichy, 29
Videla, General, 159
Viet Minh, 30–31

Vietnam, 68
Villaźon, 160

Wales, 113
Wall Street Journal, 100
Wallerstein, Immanuel, 5
Washington, D.C., 28, 129,
 133, 136, 138, 143, 160–61,
 179–80
Weathermen, 63
West Indies, 79
White House, 28
Williams, Eric, 17
Williams, P., 113
World War II, 23

Yapacaní, 167
Yungas, 146–8, 158

Zola, Emile, 23
Zurich, 97

PLUTO ⚡ PRESS

Established in 1972, Pluto Press publishes radical books across a wide range of subjects. Women in Ireland, the 1984–5 Miners' Strike in Britain, acid rain and rap music are some of the issues covered by recent books. New series include a Thriller/Crime list and Liberation Classics. Amongst our authors are Sheila Rowbotham, James Baldwin, Augusto Boal, Barbara Ehrenreich, Julian Rathbone, Claude McKay, Ariel Dorfman, Alice Miller and André Gorz.

For more information about Pluto books write to –

Pluto Press
105a Torriano Avenue
London NW5 2RX
UK

or
Pluto Press
PO Box 199
Leichhardt, NSW 2040
Australia

or
Pluto Press
51 Washington Street
Dover, New Hampshire 03820
USA